AROUND THE
WORLD
IN EASY
WAYS

Around the
World
In Easy
Ways

A Guide to Planning

Long-Term Travel

With or Without Your Kids

lisa Shusterman

First printing 2010

Although the author and publisher have made every effort to ensure the accuracy and completeness of the information contained in this book, we assume no responsibility for errors, inaccuracies, omissions, or any inconsistency herein. No portion of this book is intended to substitute for legal and/or medical advice by a qualified professional when appropriate.

Cover image provided by photocatalogs.com who retains the copyright.

Shusterman, lisa.
    Around the world in easy ways: a guide to planning long-term travel with or without your kids / by lisa Shusterman
    p.cm
    ISBN 1-44994-085-4

    1. Travel. 2. Around the world. 3. Travel with kids
I. Title.

Printed in the United States of America

This book is dedicated to my husband Marty
and my daughters Avocet and Siena,
my co-partners in this adventure
we call life.

CONTENTS

PREFACE

I'm writing this book because this is the book I wanted to read when I was planning our family's year long trip around the world. There were a plethora of guide books to tell you where to go and what to do, but I never found a "How To" book - one that would help me formulate a "To Do" list. I knew there would be a myriad of details to attend to and I was looking for guidance. Surely we were not the first family to take a year long trip and I wanted to learn what my predecessors already knew: what they had done right, and what they had done wrong. I also craved advice regarding traveling with kids beyond the borders of Europe.

I was curious as to what thoughts and feelings had gone through the minds of those who had already done this. Marty and I were a roller coaster of emotions over our 2 ½ years of planning and our year of travel. Were all of these feelings normal? Or were they signs that this was just the wrong thing to be doing? Someone else's well expressed feelings regarding a trip like this might have been a comfort.

There's another reason for writing this book. We did it! We didn't just think of this idea and sit on it, we made it happen. If our story can inspire one other person or family to live out their long term travel dream, then the purpose of writing this book will have been fulfilled.

So here's to you travelers who are thinking or fantasizing about a long term trip. May this book serve as a guide to make your life easier. St. Augustine said, "The world is a book and those who do not travel read only one page." Go forth and enjoy the Whole Book!

WHO IS THIS BOOK FOR?

If you are thinking about long term travel, this book is for you. If you are curious about how to plan a journey of this magnitude, this book is for you. Or if you want to vicariously enjoy someone else's travel adventure, this book is for you.

People are choosing to make long term travel part of their lives: empty nesters, ready to stop putting their life on hold for their kids and start living their personal dream, individuals taking a sabbatical year, those between jobs seizing the opportunity to see more of the world, homeschoolers who are incorporating extensive travel into their curriculum. Maybe hitting the road is related to your work. Maybe you don't fit into any of these categories but you've decided to live out a lifelong desire of extended travel. If you are planning a long term trip, you will find the information in this book invaluable.

Have I covered everything you will encounter during the preparation for your trip? Certainly not! Will reading this book relieve you from reading guide books or doing additional trip research? No way! I don't believe that book exists and I am certainly not going to claim that I am writing it. But, if you are planning a long journey, you will glean a multitude of ideas from reading this book, possibly many you will read nowhere else. And, you might just find yourself entertained along the way.

Chapter One

WHY WE DID IT

People thought we were crazy when we told them we were taking a year off to travel around the world. Who takes a year off to travel? I guess if we were retired with grown children and independently wealthy, they might have looked at us differently. But no, we are not retired, we have elementary school age twin daughters and we are definitely not rich. So what ever made us think of such a bizarre idea, and more importantly, what ever made us think that we could pull it off?

First of all, we are not the only ones doing long term travel. As we circumnavigated the globe, we met lots of individuals, couples and families, who were doing the exact same thing or something similar. The majority of these people were not Americans; they were from countries where their national culture is more likely to support this type of adventure, or at least, doesn't discourage it.

I grew up in a family that traveled, not extensive world travel, but we always took a three week family vacation in August. It was the old fashioned, squeeze the family into the Chrysler station wagon type of trip where you drove thousands of miles and saw the sights of our beautiful country: Yellowstone National Park, Mt. Rushmore, The Corn Palace and the World's Largest Ball of String. Often we would go to Canada as we had relatives there. But when I was nine years old, my parents took my older sister and me to Europe. It was one of those three week five country whirlwind trips, but no matter, I thought it was just way too cool. Back then, nine year old kids didn't go to Europe with the frequency that they do now. I liked trying the new foods, hearing the different languages, experiencing unique cultures and seeing things that I had only previously seen or read about in books. Upon my return, I remember wearing an

Austrian dirndl (traditional dress), purchased on the trip, to my first day of fourth grade and thinking that I was truly special.

When I got older, I took a number of trips on my own. I wish I had taken more, but I suffered from the same problem that many others suffer from: I either had time but no money or money but no time. And being the practical, rational American that I am, I couldn't seem to work through this dilemma. During the earlier days of my career, I had a client who decided that he, his wife and their nine year old daughter were going to take a year off to sail. What a marvelous, adventurous idea, I thought. Since I get sea sick, the specific idea of sailing didn't stick with me. But the idea of taking a year off to travel did.

In 1990 I met Marty, who eventually became my husband. I told him that someday I wanted to take a year off to travel. Either he liked the idea or he thought I was crazy and would never attempt to do such a thing. We married in 1992 and then life came at us fast. The next thing I knew, we had a house, a mortgage and twin girls born in 1998. The idea of a year off to travel seemed like a distant memory and hardly something that would ever happen.

But kids grow, start school and become a little more independent. I glimpsed a resurrection of my old life and in crept that crazy old one year off idea. But now we have two young children! You know, the good thing about kids is that they are not nailed to the floor. They are very portable. And if this year of travel would be exciting and enlightening for us, just think of what it would be like for Avocet and Siena (our daughters) with their whole lives ahead of them!

I thought back to my clients who were my inspiration. Their daughter was nine when they took their year off. Nine years old seems like a good age. Old enough to remember things and to gain a lot of the knowledge that a trip like this would offer. At nine, children are pretty independent, which would make our parenting a lot easier. And, our kids would still enjoy being with us; just a year or two later, they will prefer not knowing who we are (unless they need transportation or money). Summer 2008 got etched into the recesses of my mind.

In December, 2005, I said to Marty, "If we are ever going to take this trip, we better start planning it now! These kinds of things don't just happen; you have to make them happen. If we don't do this now, we probably never will." A little overly dramatic? Maybe. But that is the way I felt. I knew that a lot could happen during a 2½ year time period that might ultimately prevent us from taking this trip, but I also knew that if we didn't move forward, then our lack of initiative would prevent it. In the end, we would have no one to blame but ourselves.

So why would we want to quit our jobs, pull our kids out of school, leave behind everyone and everything we know for a life of the unknown? Our lives had become routine and somewhat predictable. There was comfort with that routine and predictability, but also a boredom and narrow mindedness. Taking a year off, a year away from our lives, was a way to break our inertia. It would create opportunities to open our minds and see things from a different perspective. And it would give us an opportunity to step away from our day to day lives and live a life different from the one we had been living. A trip like this would require us to step outside of our comfort zone and force us to stretch ourselves personally; we felt that we would all grow as individuals from such an experience.

Traveling was also a way for us to experiment with our adventurous sides. It was an opportunity to see the world, to meet new and varied people who look at life and live life in a way that is uniquely theirs. It would be a chance to experience history where it was made. When you travel you are no longer reading the book, you are the book. You are inside a National Geographic magazine.

Walking down a street in Christchurch, New Zealand, we saw a sign in a travel agent's window that summed up our feelings regarding travel:

Your Journey should open more than suitcases.

It is a rare opportunity to open doors to new cultures,

Exhilarating & liberating experiences.

This is your journey.

Form your own opinions, build your memories and enrich

Your life with the values that only come from

Broadened minds.

We really wanted to take this year long trip around the world! If we didn't do it, would we regret it later? Typically it's not the things that we do in our lives that we regret, it's the things that we don't do; we didn't want to have to face this one further down the road. We decided not to wait for a written invitation to go out and experience life; we were just going to do it!

Still, it was not an easy thing to move forward with. Marty and I were raised with a strong work ethic, with a sense that our lives should be useful, purposeful and productive. We should strive for security and, once obtained, do everything that we can to hold on to it. Chucking it all for a year of travel hardly seemed to be following the rules of our upbringing. While my father passed away six months prior to the planning stage, I could still hear his voice in my mind, "What a crazy thing to do."

Timing was another issue. My mother was older and something could happen to her while we were gone. We were concerned that at Marty's age (54), finding a job when we returned might prove challenging. And as we got closer to our departure date, the exchange rates were so poor that it appeared the trip would be way over budget. We eventually came to accept that there is no perfect time to undertake a life changing event.

As we began to tell family and friends what we were planning, we heard mixed reactions. Some thought it was totally absurd. Other were fascinated but felt that it was not something they had any desire to do. Others looked at us longingly and said, "Oh, I would love to do something like that!" I responded, "You can," but secretly wondered if they too were struggling with the same issues that Marty and I needed to overcome in order to make this happen.

Over the two plus years of planning, we revisited these issues numerous times. We began to see that they were excuses we were using to hold ourselves back from moving forward with a new chapter in our lives. We didn't have to accept the restraints that we were raised with but instead had the ability to make an alternative life choice. We started seeing ourselves as trailblazers, creating a new vision of how we could lead our lives. And, of course, our hope was that Siena and Avocet would learn that they could create a new vision of how to lead their lives.

Why We Did It

It's not that life on the road was a panacea. We encountered numerous problems while traveling. Just like at home, we had good days and bad days. We even had days when we were bored. But being bored in Jaipur, India is still a different experience than being bored in Cincinnati, Ohio. Long term travel was not an escape from our lives; it was a way to experience a different life for a short period of time. Eventually we had to come back home.

And Here is Where We Went...

Thursday, December 20, 2007
WHERE IN THE WORLD IS THE
SHUSTERMAN/GREENWELL FAMILY
Posted by lisa 11:40 AM

With less than 6 months before we leave, the countdown is on! We have about half of our accommodations booked and half of the visas that we need before we leave in our passports. We have a stack of Euros stashed away (assuming that the dollar will drop further) and we hold a FREE one way ticket to Amsterdam for all four of us (Thank you Delta Frequent Flyers).

So now you ask, "Where are we going?" If you're planning that once in a lifetime vacation (I know we are) and want to hook up with us, you'll need to know where we will be when -- so here's the rundown.

June 10-11 Dallas/Ft. Worth (Only way out on those FREE tickets)
June 12-July 2 Netherlands
July 3-July 21 Poland
July 22 Czech Republic (Only way to get to Dubrovnik cheap)
July 23-August 7 Croatia
August 8-August 25 Slovenia
August 26-September 25 Italy
September 26-October 18 Tanzania/Zanzibar
October 19-November 8 India
November 9-November 24 Thailand
November 25-December 8 Laos
December 9-December 20 Thailand (We had such a good time the first time -- we're back)

December 21-January 9 China
January 10-February 8 Australia/Tasmania
February 9-March 8 New Zealand
March 8-March 12 Tahiti
March 13-March 17 Rapa Nui (Easter Island for you
plebeians)
March 18-April 5 Chile
April 6-April 22 Argentina
April 23-May 4 Uruguay
May 5-May 25 Ecuador
May 26-June 1 Sun City Center, Florida (Bubie Stop)
June 2 Home

17 Countries, 40 Cities and One Year!

Chapter Two

FOR HOW LONG?

As we prepared for our one year odyssey, some well traveled friends asked, "Are you sure you really want to go for a full year? That's a really long time." When they go out traveling, they go for a three to four month period and feel that is more than enough. Of course, when they travel, they are on the go, non stop, for the entire three to four months – a totally different pace than we were contemplating. We acknowledged a year is a long time, but in our case, it was a time frame that made sense.

Prior to leaving, Marty worked for a small company. He was needed in his position full time, all the time. It wasn't the type of situation where he could take a six month leave, paid or unpaid, or even a three month leave. A three week vacation, maybe, but that's about it. In order to take a longer trip, it would require Marty to quit his job, not an easy thing to do unless you are independently wealthy or ready to retire – we are neither. With two nine year olds, we have lots of working years ahead of us. Once you know you have to quit your job to make this trip, you ask yourself, "Is it worth quitting and having to look for another job in order to take a three month break? How about a six month break?" The truth is, if you're going to have to look for a new job which is hard work and risky, the amount of time you take off needs to justify the action. A year, in our opinion, was just that amount of time.

Because we have kids, school was another issue to take into consideration. We could have gone away just for the summer, eleven weeks, but we had already determined that would not be worth quitting our jobs over. Once we considered going past the summer break, we needed to concern ourselves with what the school year would look like. Start the kids off in school and pull them out half way? What if they were having an awesome year?

Had just met their new best friend? Or got a lead role in the school play? Definitely not a good way to start the trip - with our kids resenting us and our dream. Working it in reverse wasn't a whole lot better. Travel for six months then put the kids back into school. Talk about feeling out of place or socially disconnected. We weren't going to be on our children's hit list with that one either.

The last school option was to homeschool the whole year and then go for whatever amount of time we desired without worrying about the school year. If we were already homeschoolers, this would have been a pretty easy choice. It fits right in with one of the reasons people choose to homeschool in the first place, flexibility. But since we weren't homeschoolers, it meant having to establish a homeschooling network and routine for a partial year. When it came down to it, taking the kids out of school for the full year proved to be the best option.

How about our home? We own a home. What were we going to do with it while we were gone? We could let the largest asset we own sit there, unattended, or have a local university student who needs a free place to live come and house sit while we were gone. But we were looking at expenses for both our travels and at home and were seeking ways to reduce costs. We didn't want to sell the house, but keeping it meant we would have to continue to pay the mortgage whether or not we were enjoying its comforts. The only way to help reduce that cost was to rent the house. Very few people are interested in a three month rental. Not a whole lot more are interested in a six month rental. Realistically speaking, you can only seriously entertain the thought of renting your home when you will be gone for at least a year. That doesn't mean it's impossible to go for a shorter period of time and still successfully rent your home, it just means it will be much more challenging finding someone to fill that niche.

Another issue factored into the equation was planning. There is a huge amount of planning and preparation to take a long trip. That is true whether it is for six months, nine months or twelve months. A large amount of the work we did in order to prepare for this trip would have been the same regardless of how long we were going.

The same is true for expenses. Certainly it costs more to travel for twelve months than it does for nine, but some expenses are fixed and cost the same either way. The suitcases we purchased, the clothes we bought, the passports we renewed, the vaccinations we obtained… all of these costs were the same regardless of how long we were gone. When you amortize the cost of these fixed expenses over a longer period of time, you can actually say that the overall trip costs less per month than a shorter trip!

Lastly, what is it we wanted to accomplish by taking this trip and how long did we need in order to achieve that goal? Leaving our life as we know it for three months would barely make a dent in our desire to live a different life for a while. For that short period, some of our friends wouldn't even realize we were gone. And, if we left over the right three months, we wouldn't have to worry about who was going to mow our lawn in our absence. To truly experience vacating our existing life, we felt a full year was needed. We would have to be gone all four seasons and be disengaged from the tasks associated with each season. To experience our entire family's "disconnect" from the kid's school, a full school year would have to be missed. And the same was true with respect to our community. A year is a long time, but we needed to be gone for a long time in order to experience a "real" change.

When you go on vacation, it takes a good week to wind down and start relaxing. Near the end of a trip, you begin to gear up for going home. We wanted an ample amount of time to live a traveler's life in between the wind down and gear up phases.

And we wanted to go all the way around the world, visiting countries on all continents. And we longed to do it at a slow and easy pace. In order to not be on the go all the time and to cover a lot of territory, we needed time. If you are willing to pick up the pace or forego some destinations, you can consider a shorter trip; we were not.

In the end, was a year too long? Yes and no. Our pace worked well for us. If we had shortened our travel time, we would have had to cut out some of our itinerary. But at the ten month point a definite shift had occurred – a shift of being tired and ready to go home. We had two other factors occurring at the same time, making it difficult to pinpoint the true cause of our weariness.

Avocet and Siena's good friends from the US had moved to Chile for a two year period. Our plan was to visit with them for ten days once we hit South America – close to our ten month point. It was a great visit but once the visit was over, Siena and Avocet looked at us and said, "Now we want to go home." The let down after the visit was tremendous and most definitely was an influencing factor on our feelings at the time.

The other issue occurring simultaneously was where we were in our itinerary. We were not as thrilled with our choice of locations in South America as we had been on other continents. At first we were chalking up our disappointment to the fact that it was the end of the trip and everyone was just ready to go home. But then, our very last destination, Quito, Ecuador was great. We all loved it. So what happened to the rationale that it was the end of the trip and everyone was ready for home? Maybe these feelings of wanting to go back home weren't about being out too long after all.

If we were to do it again would we go out for a year? If all the factors involved in making our decision in the first place were equal, the answer would be yes. If we didn't have the same issues to consider: job, owning a home, school etc. I would choose to go for about a nine to ten month period and shorten the itinerary to fit that time frame. Marty, on the other hand, says he would go out for two years or maybe even three.

A Glimpse of Life at Nine Weeks...

Wednesday, August 6, 2008
LIFE ON THE ROAD
Posted by lisa at 3:27 AM

We are now in our ninth week of travel. Prior to this trip, the longest Marty had been away at one time was three weeks. I had been away for six weeks in Israel and Greece, but that was combined with visiting family. Life on the road can be fun and exciting but also tiring, frustrating and even boring sometimes. There are lots of surprises – both good and bad, and many things to be grateful for.

Having only one 28" rolling duffel bag per person, every item put into those bags was well thought out. I am pleased to say that so far, we feel that everything that we have brought has been needed and that we are not finding ourselves lacking for anything. Bored with what we have maybe, but not lacking.

We left with a "well stocked" first aid kit (within reason) and I feel grateful that to date, we have needed nothing beyond a Motrin or two and Neosporin for a cut Siena obtained while climbing rocks.

Our first two apartments (six weeks total) had internet access and we came to love the convenience that it offered. Now, without it in Korcula, Croatia, we feel frustrated, irritated and put out. We have an internet cafe $\frac{1}{2}$ hour away but it's definitely not the same. It's amazing how addicted to technology we are and how "disconnected" we can feel when we don't have it. If you check our blog regularly, you noticed a week long gap where we didn't post anything. It was not from lack of interest but lack of opportunity. We missed writing and the intellectual stimulation that it can bring.

We all love each other very much but when you talk with the same three people all the time, you start to get tired of them. Our ears are constantly perked for any sound of the English language and we attack the source in hopes of a conversation with someone else. Unfortunately, they haven't necessarily been deprived of conversation for quite as long and may not be as desperate as we are.

Travel days are tough. Even if everything goes smoothly, they are still tough. You are giving up the comfort and familiarity of a place you have come to love and don't necessarily want to leave. You are heading to a place that will hopefully be exciting, but you really don't know for sure what it will be like. And you have to "figure out" everything from the beginning: transportation system, language, where to buy food, your way around town, etc. It's interesting but it is work and sometimes complacency seems a better alternative.

To date, we have taken three flights, one long distance train, and a long distance ferry. All of our baggage has arrived at our destination intact. We count our blessings each time we see those four bags on a baggage claim conveyor belt.

Every place we have been to, we have felt perfectly safe for both our personal beings as well as our possessions. Nothing has ever been taken from us and never once have we felt in danger of any theft. Here on Korcula, we don't even lock our door at night.

A lot of times you have everything you need, just not always at the same time. In Krakow, Poland, we had a coffee maker and filters but had run out of decaf coffee (I can only drink decaf) and couldn't find any. Right before leaving Krakow, we found some decaf and bought extra to take with us to Croatia. In Dubrovnik, we had the coffee and coffee maker but no filters. Couldn't find any filters in the store so we bought paper towels to use for filters. By the time we got to Korcula, we had decaf coffee but no coffee maker and no filters, only an espresso pot. When life gives you an espresso pot, you learn to make espresso!

Whether, it's moving from home to home or just on a day trip, there's always the risk of losing things. So far our record isn't too bad. Marty lost his baseball cap which has now been replaced by a panama hat (he looks quite debonair). We lost one Nalgene water bottle in the Krakow airport when we were there to pick up my mother – we are making do with just three bottles. The worst was also at the Krakow airport at the same time as the water bottle loss. Avocet left her brand new purse (purchased in Zakopane) in the bathroom at the airport and by the time she realized it, it was gone. Financially, it was not a great loss but emotionally it was huge!

We spend a lot of time being versus doing. If we were Buddhists, we would be right up there with the Enlightened. But we're Americans, where what we do and accomplish is how we judge and value ourselves, it's a tough transition. At times we feel unproductive and a little at a loss. We start to wonder what our purpose is – of course that is all part of this process that we call travel but it sure feels uncomfortable.

Some days the exotic is no longer appealing and we long for easy and familiar – our own bed and pillow, jam the flavor we want and not just what's available, a stove that cooks with even heat and a refrigerator that actually keeps things cold instead of just cool. Other days, the view of the Adriatic Sea off the balcony makes all those other "things" insignificant.

Our day to day life is very much about what we create for ourselves. There isn't a whole lot that we have to "react" to – no work, few time constraints, no extra curricular activities, no school or volunteer obligations...the list goes on and on. It's a freedom that we all longed for and yet, ironically, it comes with a lot of responsibility. What strange lives we lead.

And Another Glimpse at Six Months...

Wednesday, December 10, 2008
<u>SIX MONTH STATE OF THE UNION</u>
Posted by lisa at 4:11 AM

As of today, December 10th, we have been on the road for six months or one half of our trip. On one hand, it feels like it was not that long ago that we were sitting in the Dallas-Fort Worth Airport waiting to leave the US. On the other hand, it feels like a lifetime ago. Time is a very funny thing. Overall, it seems that the second three months have passed much faster than the first three months. I'm not sure if that trend will continue for the next six months or not.

At this point we are $\frac{3}{4}$ the way through what we perceived to be our toughest countries. We knew that Europe, Australia and New Zealand would be the easiest places. Africa, India, Thailand, Laos and China would be the toughest. And the countries of South America, somewhere in between. Europe was in fact very easy, but as it turns out, so was Thailand and Laos. Africa was not what I would call easy, but much easier than expected. Only India was in fact as challenging as what we had predicted. I'm guessing that China will be that way as well.

On the road we don't take anything for granted and we have much to be thankful for. At this point we have had thirteen flights which have all landed safely and our luggage has always been there waiting for us. We have not missed any trains, planes, ferries, buses or other forms of transportation and nothing has been more than two hours late and has never been a hardship. We were out of India by

16

the time of the Mumbai bombings, and out of Thailand before the Bangkok Airport closed and things got intense there. We are now back in Thailand for eleven days with a flight scheduled out on December 21st and at the moment it looks as if flights will be leaving Bangkok as scheduled.

We have all had days where we are "tired of traveling" but then we seem to be able to snap out of it after a short while. Avocet and Siena say they "miss home" with a certain amount of frequency with the specifics usually being: their friends, the house and their stuff. They make no mention of missing school. Marty misses his friends and his car and me, well, I miss my friends but that's about it. We are all longing to get back to apartments! We have managed in guesthouses/hotels fine and have learned to make common areas our "living room," but we really miss having a kitchen. It's nice when someone else cooks and cleans up for you but it really gets old eating in restaurants. We wonder if we'll ever eat in any restaurants in Sydney after having had to do it for four months!

Everyone has been healthy (another thing we are thankful for) with the exception of an occasional tummy ache or headache. This is particularly significant at this stage of the trip as we had assumed that we would all have gotten sick in Africa and/or India. Our first aid kit is intact with the exception of the use of some bandaids, antiseptic ointment, Advil, Dramamine and an occasional OTC sleeping aid. It would be nice if we could come home with the kit looking the way it does right now. We have less than a month more of taking our Malerone (anti-maleria) pills and will all be happy to stop taking them. Fortunately, we have not had any "known" side effects.

I try to think of how we have all changed, for certainly after an adventure like this, we are bound to change. We've watched Avocet and Siena blossom into amazing beings; they are sophisticated way beyond their years. We all see how we can live with a lot less than what we are used to, not unlike the many people we see in the countries we are traveling in. It's clear to us that relationships are what life is all about. It's what we miss most from home and what we so much enjoy in our travels. And having been in Buddhist countries for the past month, learning and living the concept that the past is over and done and the present is what we have, will be something that we will continue to strive toward. My guess is that all the ways in which we have changed won't be apparent until after we get back home.

Even after six months on the road, sometimes we have to pinch ourselves and say, yes, this is really happening. We are here in Thailand, half way around the world and spending a year of our lives traveling. It's hard to believe it now and I'm sure when we return home it will all seem like a dream.

Chapter Three

HOW MANY RUPEES WILL YOU NEED?

The number one question contemplated by all, but asked by none, as we prepared to go was "How can they afford this?" The reason no one asked us this is because in America, it is just not polite to talk about money. Therefore, the question was not asked to us, just about us. Friends would ask this question to other friends. Those who knew my mother would ask her. People speculated about the cost of this adventure and how it was possible we could afford such an "extravagant" trip. Only one friend, right before leaving, was brave enough to actually confront me and ask me to my face, "How much is this going to cost you?" My reply, "Not as much as you think."

We live in a very nice home, in a very nice neighborhood in the very affordable city of Cincinnati. We drive a ten year old minivan and a four year old Toyota Matrix. Our children go to public school and Marty's favorite clothing store is the local thrift shop. We are far from poor, but we are hardly what I would call rich. We make very conscious choices about how we spend our money, making sure our resources go to the things in life that are important to us. Travel is one of those areas we deem important.

Taking this trip was not a spur of the moment thing. It was a seed planted in my brain almost 20 years ago. I can't say we've been consciously saving for this trip that long, but certainly, saving is in both my and my husband's nature. So money had been meticulously saved for years: for retirement, college education, a rainy day, or maybe even a rainy (or not so rainy) year. When in 2006 we decided to attempt to make this trip a reality by June 2008, we knew money was not going to be what would hold us back.

19

Around the World in Easy Ways

There are all different ways of traveling, something available for every budget. We are not the camping, eating take away out of the supermarket kind of family, but neither are we resort type people. We are somewhere in between. And, of course, there is a lot of somewhere in between. Estimates were calculated, budgets were set, we knew some countries would be more expensive than others and some events would be worth splurging for.

Airfares were one of the two largest line items in our budget. We needed to get four people all the way around the world, crossing hemispheres multiple times and traveling within the Southern Hemisphere which is more expensive than air travel in the Northern Hemisphere. After putting together our itinerary, we spoke to a Round the World Broker. While exact prices could not be quoted at the time, we were given an estimate of about $26,000-$28,000, an average of up to $7,000 per person. In the end, our airfares came in at $30,000, an average of $7,500 per person. When you think about what an airfare can cost, round trip, to get to just one country; Australia, New Zealand or China, $7,500 per person is not really all that bad. And there are definitely ways to do it cheaper. We were told at the outset, if we skip South America, it will be a lot cheaper; air travel there is very expensive. But in our minds, how can you skip an entire continent? There were also times we flew some place where we could have opted to take a long bus ride, but since three out of four of us get bus sick, we figured the extra money spent was well worth it.

While we spent money on an extra air fare here and there, by planning the trip in advance, we were able to save a lot of money, being more organized about our travel. We would meet travelers who hop scotched around, back tracking and circling, creating a need for more flights than would otherwise be required to cover the same countries. We were also able to take advantage of air broker discounts by advance planning. We paid for one flight from Auckland, New Zealand to Buenos Aires, Argentina, which enabled us to stop in Tahiti, Rapa Nui, Chile, and Santiago, Chile. I'm not talking about a stop over, I'm talking about anywhere from an eight to a twenty one day stay in each of the three locations, all on one airfare!

The next biggest line item in the budget was accommodations. We set a goal for ourselves that we wanted to

20

spend, on average, no more than $100 US per night. This was for two or three bedroom apartments for eight months and guest houses or hotels for the other four months. Some countries would be pricier than others, but we were looking at averages. In the end, our average came out to be $97 US per night. At the high end was our $200+ per night stay in a hotel in Hong Kong and at the low end was our $16 per night stay in a hotel in Jaipur, India. Trying to keep costs low? Choose shorter stays in expensive cities and longer stays in cities that offer a bargain.

The final cost of the trip came in at (drum roll please), $118,600. This included everything! It included any clothes specifically purchased for the trip, new suitcases and backpacks, passports, visas, vaccinations, new cameras, a used laptop, accommodations, international health insurance, eating out, eating in, sightseeing activities, trains, planes and automobiles... It really included everything! It even included splurges like a five day safari in Tanzania ($3800), swimming with the dolphins and a whale watch in New Zealand, a full day weaving class in Laos and a two day trip to Iguazu Falls in Argentina. When we were estimating what the whole trip would cost, we estimated $250 per day plus airfare. This was a somewhat arbitrary figure based on the $100 per day accommodation allowance plus a per day estimate of everything else. Since we were gone 358 days (one week shy of a full year), 358 X $250 = $89,500 + $30,000 = $119,500. Pretty darn good estimating!

Can it be done for less? Yes, without even trying really hard. Avoid the splurges, eat in all the time instead of eating in restaurants, take fewer flights and use more overland transportation (which is not always a guarantee of saving money), don't buy any souvenirs, don't ship home the souvenirs you're not buying, stay in less expensive accommodations, spend more time in India or Southeast Asia, skip Europe. You will have to weigh what is more important to you and what is not a high priority and then make your decisions from that point.

We wanted our accommodations to be clean, comfortable and convenient; they were far from four stars. We ate in our apartments a lot, typically breakfast and dinner, often eating lunch in restaurants when we were out and about. Sometimes we would pack lunches. If there was a free day at a museum, we would take advantage of that and only chose to go to museums we really wanted to see, not the ones we felt we "should." You can take advantage of free activities: parks and outdoor concerts, street festivals etc. While we did all that, we also recognized we may never be back this way again. Go to Africa and not do a safari? It just didn't resonate with us. Stay in Buenos Aires, close to Iguazu Falls and not see it? It seemed like it would be a missed opportunity. But certainly, you can make choices that make it more affordable.

What the $118,600 did not include are costs associated with home. While it included our international health insurance policy, it did not include the catastrophic health insurance policy we maintained for home in order to provide us continuous coverage back here in the US. It also did not include the monthly mortgage on our house or any household related expenses such as utilities (water only) and insurance. We stored our cars in our own garage (which we did not rent with the house) but still had to maintain a minimal amount of insurance on them in case of theft. Some of these expenses were offset by the fact we rented our house and that our renters paid for all of their utilities other than water.

Before you start looking at these figures and shaking your head that this is a financial impossibility for you, you need to consider all the things you are not spending money on over the course of the year. I'm talking about the cost of living at home. In our case, this included: food, eating out, vacations, entertainment (movies, theater tickets, ball game tickets, concerts, etc.), summer camps, clothing, violin rental and lessons, dance classes, skiing lessons, gasoline for our cars, phone, cell phones, utilities on the house... Have you ever really thought about how much it costs to live? If you add up all the expenses you won't have for a year and subtract it from the cost of life on the road for a year, you will discover that your year abroad is just not as expensive as you think; it may even prove to be cheaper!

The biggest expense of traveling is not what you are spending; it is what you are not earning by being gainfully employed for the year. This is the BIG THING, the SCARY THING! The thing that bucks the American way of life. Keep in mind you are not giving up your whole salary, only that portion you actually get to keep. You have this gross salary figure (what you would tell someone you make if they were rude enough to ask). But you really don't get to keep all of that, do you? The

Federal Government gets some and the State Government and even your City Government gets a piece of the action. Social Security wants their share as does Medicare. And, if you are paying for a portion of your health insurance, you don't get to keep that money either. You end up with a net figure - the amount written on your paycheck. That is the amount you are giving up. Still a huge loss, but maybe not as big as you first thought when you were thinking in gross terms.

Actually, the annual loss of income can be quantified. The big expense that can't be quantified is how long you will have to go without a job once you return home. We met some travelers from Paris who were also traveling for a year. They left their job, but upon their return, jobs will be there waiting for them. Wouldn't that be grand! If you have a place of employment that can offer you that security, then my only question to you is "What are you waiting for?" We were not in that fortuitous a position. Marty quit his job in order to make this trip and just now has found another at five months post trip. We also were not expecting to be coming back to this difficult economy (late 2009). Three months into our trip, the US declared itself in a full blown recession, the stock market sinking and unemployment rising.

In many ways, it was a great year to be gone, just not a great time to be coming back. But even with this unknown, we were still willing to move forward. Marty and I think of ourselves as bright, creative, capable people with a good work ethic and had a strong desire to make this trip happen. We figured that when we returned, we would be able to generate an income some way, somehow. It may have meant not working our first choice of jobs, but we were willing to do what we had to do – it seemed a small price to pay for having this one year adventure with our family.

Don't Forget to Budget For...

Friday, September 19, 2008
PAYING TO PEE
Posted by lisa at 8:00 AM

At the risk of dating myself, I remember pay toilets in the United States. You would go to a public restroom and there would be a contraption on the door of each stall in which you would insert a dime and turn the knob in order to be able to open the door. If you didn't have a dime, you were out of luck. Unless of course you were small, in which case you could crawl under the door, use the facilities, and then exit the normal way. The other option was to wait until someone else came out of a stall and hope that they would be willing to let you enter the stall without having to pay (even though they had to pay to get in).

It's been many years since any of us have had to pay to pee in the US. That is not the case here in Europe. In fact, finding any public bathroom facility in Europe can be challenging regardless of whether you are willing to pay or not. It is always best to first follow your mother's advice and to pee before you leave the house - this buys you at least several hours. Using the facilities in any restaurant you eat in (only available to patrons) or museum you visit is also a wise choice. But again, these still may not be free even though you have just paid for a meal or paid a large admission price to go to the museum.

Most pay toilets in Europe involve a person sitting at the entrance collecting money. The advantage of this is that exact change is not required. The disadvantage, of course, is that you can't pile yourself and your two kids into one stall for the price of one. You therefore have to pay 2E (.50E each) for your family of four to pee. That's $3.00 US for the privilege of eliminating the 12E ($18 US) worth of soft drinks that you had for lunch (yes, that is only one soft drink per person). Occasionally there is just a change bowl with a sign posted of how much it is to use the facilities. Then you have the moral dilemma of whether to follow local custom and pay, to pay, but less than full price, or to skip paying and deal with your conscience later.

The ultimate pay toilet we encountered was in the parking lot just outside the city of San Gimignano in Tuscany. It was a large modern metal structure, but only one toilet for men/women/handicapped. You inserted your .50E and the door slid open like one of the doors on the Star Ship Enterprise on Star Trek. Everything else was automatic as well. You used the toilet and then pushed a button for ten sheets of toilet paper to come through a slot. You walked over to a trough looking area and stuck your hands in. Soap was automatically dispensed. Move down the line and water was dispensed. Moving down the line further, warm air was blown in order to dry your hands. In the end you pushed a button and the door slid open again. You had a total of fifteen minutes to do your business. We were never quite clear what would happen if you exceeded your fifteen minutes. Would the door slide open and expose you to the world if you were not yet through? Once you were out, you heard a flush of water - I think some type of system washed the whole bathroom before the next person. The whole thing was rather bizarre and a little space age. The good news is that a family of four could easily fit in as long as no one was too modest. In fact, two families of four could easily have fit in the large space with a net cost of .06 1/4 E (9 cents US) per person. What a deal!

Chapter Four

CHOOSING YOUR PACE

Choosing your pace and selecting your itinerary are closely related. Some locations will work better than others with the pace you select. It may mean you have to give up the idea of going some place you have always wanted to go to because it doesn't work into your pace – oh well! You are going to lots of wonderful places no matter what. Malaysia is not disappearing. If you don't make it this time, there is always next time. Even if you never make a trip of this magnitude again, if you love to travel, you will travel another time. Maybe Malaysia will be the first place you go after this once in a lifetime trip.

Your pace will depend on:

> ➢ Your temperament
> ➢ The temperament of those traveling with you
> ➢ Whether you are traveling with children
> ➢ How long you will be gone altogether
> ➢ Which is more important: sites or culture

If you are anywhere near my age, you'll remember a movie called "If It's Tuesday, This Must Be Belgium." This 1969 movie was about a tour group on the go all the time; they didn't have time to breathe or to even think about where it was they were. They had one site after another shoved down their throats. Yes, they had been to seven European countries in eighteen days but what did they remember of each of these seven countries? As we were planning this trip, I knew one thing for sure, I didn't want our trip to look anything like that!

We acknowledged that when you spend a year on the road, it's your life, not a vacation. There are things you will need to do

26

with your time other than sightseeing - "life stuff": laundry, food shopping, communications, research, trip planning, and homework. All these things take time away from your "visiting" time. And, if you want to "live" in a city versus just being a tourist, you need extra time for that as well.

Then there's the issue of how many times do you want to pack and unpack. Exactly how many days of your trip do you want to use for travel days? Even moving a short distance can eat away an entire day when you have to travel on train or bus schedules not specifically designed for you.

Our original plan was to spend three weeks in each location. This would give us enough time to really get to know a place. We wouldn't just be passing through, we would be living there. Three weeks would give us plenty of time to do our "life stuff" without having to miss sights that area had to offer. We could take each day at a leisurely pace, going out and doing maybe one or two things a day and then have time to relax. We could take day trips to explore areas within close proximity. And we would have time to enjoy not just the touristy things, but also things that were for the locals.

As we began to formulate our itinerary, people would ask where we were going and how long we would be there. If we would say," We're going to Krakow, Poland for three weeks," they would say, "Oh, Krakow is a lovely city. You'll love it. But three or four days is more than enough." We heard that repeatedly about a number of cites we were planning to visit. Well, we spent three full weeks in Krakow and loved it. We had plenty of time to explore all the tourist sites the city had to offer without any sense of urgency. We took a day trip to Weilecka to tour the famous salt mine. Another day we spent visiting the sobering site of the concentration camp at Auschwitz. A third day trip, to the city of Zakopane in the Tatra Mountains, was so delightful; we turned the day trip into a spontaneous overnight. We rented bikes and rode around the Planty, the green space surrounding the old city. We enjoyed the International Street Performers Festival and The Jewish Festival. On one rainy day, we spent hours in Masolit, an English language bookstore which was so enjoyable we made a point of returning before we left town. The people who live in Krakow don't seem to feel three weeks is too many weeks to be there, so why should we?

27

Not all locations fit this model. I have always wanted to go to Turkey. Turkey was on our "A" list when we were choosing our itinerary. But no matter how we looked at it, we couldn't make Turkey work. There was no one city in Turkey we wanted to spend three weeks in. There were lots of amazing sites to see, but they were very spread out – Turkey is a big country! It didn't fit the model we had set up for ourselves. We decided Turkey would have to wait until another time.

We pretty much stuck to the three week model through Europe, but once we started planning Africa, we had trouble making the model work for us. Africa is a huge continent and everything is very far apart. Transportation between these places is challenging. Even though we narrowed it down to Tanzania, it was still difficult finding cities or towns where we wanted to spend more than a week. So we gave in and shortened our stays to one week. We continued at the faster pace for six weeks, through Africa and India. It was tough. We were tired of packing, unpacking and moving. And, in that time, we found there were a number of places where we would have liked to stay longer than just the one week we had planned.

When we experienced one week stays, they were often exhausting and stressful. There was always a lot we wanted to see and do and trying to squeeze it into one week along with the usual "life stuff" made for long, tiring days. It helped that these one week stays were in locations where we were not doing our own cooking, so we didn't have to fit the additional tasks of food shopping and preparation into our already overfilled schedule. In the end I had wished that almost all of our one week stays had been two weeks long.

After a series of one week stays, two weeks in Chiang Mai, Thailand seemed like a luxury. Once again it felt like there was time to just relax and enjoy, and we were happy not to be on the road quite so frequently. We never regretted any of our three week stays and our two week stays were also perfect. But almost all our one week stays were too short putting too much strain on our lives. Lengthening them to even ten days would have been an improvement.

Unless you are a person who needs to be on the go all the time or is only happy when "seeing the sights," longer stays have much to offer. They give everyone the opportunity to not just do, but to be. They offer a civilized pace to enjoy all your location has to offer, ample time to do your "life stuff" and an opportunity to relax. Meals become events when you don't have to rush off to the next activity. And there's plenty of time to experience the culture of that particular country; travel, after all, is not a composite of tourist sights! Longer stays afford you time for "real life" activities: spending time in the park where you get a real sense of local life, browsing a bookshop, boating on a lake, getting to know the local merchants. They give you time to settle in and call that city home.

If you are traveling with young children, longer stays, in my opinion, are a necessity. Despite their apparent unlimited energy, they will tire of a fast pace much sooner than you. They need breaks and good old fashioned play time. In their eyes, time on the playground at the local park with a picnic lunch may be a perfect way to spend the day. Only a longer stay will enable you to take time to do something like that without feeling you are missing something you should be seeing. Avocet and Siena enjoy a good museum as much as anyone, but not several in a row. Their drive to see and/or do was not the same as ours. Given we were a team, we had to move at the pace of the slowest members of the team. Unless we had short stays, it was never a problem to move at the slower pace – in fact, it was just perfect.

How Many of These Kind of Days Do You Want?

Thursday, July 31, 2008
TRAVEL DAYS
Posted By Marty at 2:30 AM

Travel days can be tough. Let me explain why.
When lisa did the original planning, Sky Europe, a European
discount airline, offered a flight from Krakow, Poland to
Dubrovnik, Croatia. That's one of the reasons that Croatia
became part of the itinerary. Sky Europe then moves their
operations out of Poland. Oops!!! This was six months or more
ago. lisa then finds the closest (reasonable) flight to
Dubrovnik which turns out to be out of Prague. No big deal
because the flight to Dubrovnik is only ninety minutes long.
Alright, she plans a train from Krakow to Prague. Done deal!!!
Just wait!!

It's late the night before we leave for Prague. Our landlord
has not been the best at replying to our e-mails so we aren't
sure whether his mother-in-law will show up at 5:40 AM as
planned. See, we need to catch the 5:57 AM tram across the
city to meet the 7:00 train. I thought scheduling time would
be essentially over when I retired. No way!! Mom-in-law did
show up as promised, lisa handed her the key and we were
off. Our train compartment was shared with two very nice
Jesuit priests from California, Fathers Jim and Bill. We
spent seven hours with them reading, journaling, swapping
stories, etc. We also had a nice tablecloth breakfast in the
dining car which seemed SO luxurious. And it wasn't
expensive.

We arrived in Prague at 2:00 PM to find very few signs
directing us to where the taxis were stationed. I eventually

found the tourist information booth and they pointed us to the taxi waiting area. "Fair Taxi" was the tourist info lady's choice for a reputable company and informed us we shouldn't have to pay more than 400 Koruna (about $30.00 US) to get to our hotel near the airport. When we rounded the corner we found no "Fair Taxi" and only two cabs. I like to envision them both saying "We got some suckers now". The first quoted 800 kn and the next 1000 kn. You see, Prague taxis are notorious for ripping off tourists and their countrymen alike. It's said even the Czechs hate them! One said to lisa as she walked away "What do you want to pay? like this was a marketplace. lisa said 400 kn and he said forget it.

My frustration level, already running high, helps direct me down the stairs to the metro area. Oh, by the way, "down the stairs" literally means down the stairs, no ramps, escalators, or elevators here. So I end up schlepping four heavy suitcases from one level to another. I go back to the same nice woman in the tourist information kiosk to find out that we can go three stops on the metro then take tram 22 to near our spot. She approximates on the map where our hotel is. We metro three stops then spend a lot of time finding out where the trams are, shuttling luggage and making sure the kids aren't left alone. I make sure we are on the right side of the street (remember trams go both ways...you can end up on the other side of town if you take it east vs. west).

Finally, we get on tram 22. We discover, after leaving the tram that we got off several stops too early. I walked into a manicure salon and asked where we were. The receptionist gives me a quizzical look and says in perfect Czech "§˘4€ŠĆ...etc, etc.", (no clue). I ask an older lady at the tram stop, who I have zero faith in knowing any English and she instructs us which stop to get off at. She knows where the hotel is. Go figure. We finally arrive, frazzled but okay. The girls have been troopers. Though some arguing has occurred, they have been great. Avocet and Siena would often just lie down and use their suitcases as pillows and rest while we tried to figure out what we were going to do.

The next morning the front desk clerk bangs on our door at 3:00 AM. We need to be at the airport no later than 4:00 AM to be on the 6:00 flight. We got on the plane and had an uneventful flight until the landing which was the worst I have ever experienced. Dubrovnik's airport is between the mountains and the sea and the very high winds that day made it especially bad. After doing a one wheeled landing, everyone cheered!! We collected our luggage and proceeded to ask a policeman if the bus into the city was less expensive than a taxi. If you haven't guessed, we are getting leery of taxis. He said the taxi would be "WAY MORE EXPENSIVE". We took a bus into the city only to find that very few street signs exist in Dubrovnik. I had to walk up to a business and see what the address is and compare that to the map we printed off supplied by our future landlord. Our map was not detailed and only had the large streets. We were lost! We lugged the four suitcases up the streets looking for a landmark, or something.

Finally, lisa goes off on her own, finds a gentleman who says it's up the street we are already on and to the right. After another ten minutes of walking and thinking we are getting nowhere, we arrive at our place, exhausted but home.

NEXT TIME WE SPLURGE ON THE OVERPRICED CABBIE!

Chapter Five

WHERE IN THE WORLD
DO YOU WANT TO GO?

Now that you have decided you are going to take this extended trip, where are you going to go? Even if you decide to take a full year to travel the world, it's a big world out there and you're still going to have to narrow down your itinerary. Are there places you have always wanted to go? Are there people along the way whom you want to visit? Is there a particular activity that is a must for a given family member?

Other than the wants, the needs must be kept in mind. Do you need to keep within a specific budget, making some countries unaffordable? If so, you won't be spending two weeks in Hong Kong! What about time of year and weather? Beijing in January? Will a particular location fit into the pace you have chosen for yourselves?

Who gets to decide on the itinerary? Everyone? Or just some of the people going?   In our house, Mom and Dad designed the itinerary. We figured we were able to factor in the multitude of variables required in order to make that type of decision.   In our minds, there were going to be plenty of opportunities for the girls to do trip planning within the countries chosen, so it wasn't really necessary for them to be a part of the initial trip itinerary process. If I had to do it over again, I would do it differently and let them help. As long as they fully understood that just because they picked a place they wanted to go, that it wasn't necessarily going to become a reality, making them part of the itinerary process might have created more buy in from the beginning.

On New Year's Day, 2006, 2½ years prior to our envisioned departure date, I made a list of all the places I would like to go.

Independently, Marty made a list of his places. We sat down and compared notes. Any place on both lists stayed. If a country appeared on only one list, then it was open for discussion. If there was strong opposition (like I had zero desire to go to Iceland) then that country was dropped; if it was not objectionable than it stayed. From here, the real work began.

Marty and I each picked a country and started researching it. We chose to use travel books from the library to avoid the huge expense that would be associated with buying a book for each country we wanted to explore. These were not necessarily the most current books, but for this purpose, that wasn't important. We also opted for books instead of the Internet since books are portable and we could take the books everywhere we might want to work. It was also helpful to have a travel book format for our initial explorations. Armed with library material, we read and read and read. We looked for places that resonated with us, locations where we felt we would want to settle in for a while and cities where there were places to see and things to do that would interest us. We knew we would be interested in experiencing different cultures and we wanted to explore all the continents.

I found books that covered regions versus just one country to be particularly helpful at the beginning. Some of our favorite destinations were discovered this way; places that had never even appeared on our original "A" list. We knew we wanted to explore some countries in Eastern Europe, listing Bulgaria and Croatia originally. While reading a guidebook on Eastern Europe, I started perusing the section on Slovenia. Ljubljana, Slovenia became a three week stay on our final itinerary and we all loved it. The same thing happened in Southeast Asia. Our original list contained Thailand, Vietnam and Cambodia. But while looking at a book on Southeast Asia, a chapter on Laos caught my attention big time. Luang Prabang was a highlight of our stay in that part of the world. My point is, don't limit your explorations to the countries on your "A" list; use that as a guide and let your research take you anywhere. Take your time and keep an open mind.

Flow was very important as we were trying to finalize our itinerary. How are you going to get from point A to point B? Will that trip be easy? Or a challenge? Will it be cost effective or blow the budget. We all wanted to go to Greece, but it seemed too trying to get there from where we were. After exploring all the transportation options, we gave up on Greece. Our philosophy was, "If it was too much of a struggle to make it happen, let it go." We had a similar situation with Dubrovnik, Croatia. Dubrovnik is supposed to be absolutely beautiful! (and it is). But it is at the very bottom of Croatia, a long, skinny country. Flights were expensive. We could take the bus from Ljubljana to Zagreb and then catch the train to Split. From Split, we could either take a bus or a ferry to Dubrovnik. It would have required an overnight in Zagreb (expensive and not very exciting). We finally chalked it up as too much of a struggle and let it go. But sometimes when you let things go, they come back to you. At a future point we added Krakow, Poland to our itinerary (another country not on the "A" list but picked up from a regional guidebook). Sky Europe airline just so happened to have a cheap flight from Krakow to Dubrovnik. Croatia here we come.

If you are going to use a Round the World Airline Ticket, that will have a major impact on your itinerary. You are often limited to a certain number of stops and depending on your ticket, certain locations. You need to continue in the direction you first chose (always east or always west) and some tickets put a restriction on the number of miles you can cover. Be sure to check all the rules and restrictions to any ticket you consider.

Cost can be a huge factor in determining your itinerary. We met many travelers who were going around the world but who were not going to Europe. Did they dislike European countries? No, they disliked the costs associated with those countries. At the time we were traveling, the Euro was high. For travelers outside of Europe, it made traveling to those countries very expensive. One of the best ways to extend your "travel dollars" is to avoid expensive countries and spend more time in cheaper ones. We could have lived in SE Asia for a year for what it cost us to spend just three months in Europe – and we were in some "less" expensive places in Europe. Lots of travelers spend an entire year in Southeast Asia as they can do it for far less than what it costs them to live at home. We went for the balancing effect. Yes, we went to Venice where a soft drink cost $6.50 US. But then we went to Mcleodganj, India where that same $6.50 US bought a meal, with drinks, for our entire family of four. Our apartment in Krakow cost $1030 US per week, but our apartment in Quito, Ecuador cost $180 US per week. There's no question about it, you can travel longer for less money by sticking to less expensive countries.

When looking at costs, you must consider exchange rates, which will change over your planning period and the course of your trip. Accept the fact from the beginning that you're not in control of what happens to the dollar (or whatever currency is your home currency) and then let it go. Some exchange rates will work in your favor and some will work against you. Just hope there is some justice in this world and that it will all balance out. By the time we left the US for Europe, the US Dollar was at its lowest point in years. We watched the Euro rise against the Dollar each day for months but we knew we were too far into this project to change our plans. Needless to say, Europe ended up costing us more than we had planned. Six months later we were in Australia and New Zealand where the Dollar had climbed dramatically against their currency. These two "expensive countries" turned out to be unexpected bargains.

Weather is another factor that will play a key role in helping to formulate your itinerary. Trying to keep to milder temperatures definitely makes for an easier time packing and for some (like me who hates the cold) an awesome year of an eternal spring. What about rainy seasons? Nothing like being in a great city during their rainy season to dampen your spirit (pun intended). Perfect weather everywhere cannot be had. That doesn't mean you can't strive for it. We opted to head east, hitting Europe in the summer. As fall approached, we popped down to Africa where the temperatures are pretty consistent year round, but where it would be dry, and then over to India, where temperatures would be slightly cooler in the fall than they would be during the summer. We spent the latter part of autumn and early winter in Southeast Asia for continued mild temperatures and then wintered in the Southern Hemisphere where we could have summer all over again. When it looked like we would hit Thailand before the rainy season was over, we added extra time to our European itinerary so we would hit Thailand a few weeks later.

While weather should play a role in your planning, keep in mind that weather is a lot like exchange rates – you have no control over it. And as we used to say in the investment industry, past performance is no guarantee of future performance. Realizing we would be in China in December, we opted to stay in the south for its historically mild temperatures. We arrived to Yangshou expecting daytime temps in the 60's. That's what the historical averages indicated. Instead we found daytime temps in the low 40's and people telling us how beautiful it was the week before we got there. In the sixteen days we spent in Yangshou, only two hit their "average" highs. When life gives you lemons, make lemon gelato.

Weather timing is not the only timing to look at when planning a particular location. Look at the timing of national or local festivals you might want to try to participate in. You won't be able to catch each one, but you can certainly aim for them if you know they exist. We were able to catch the Euro Cup finals while in Europe, the Jewish Festival and International Street Performers Festival in Poland, Diwali in India, Loy Krathong in Thailand, Australia Day in... There may also be holidays and festivals you want to avoid either because everything in town will be closed or the city will be too crowded. Some holidays are neither to be strived for nor avoided, just planned for. We were going to be in Zanzibar during Ramadan, a time which the Islamic faithful fast for a month. We took extra care in making sure we would find places to eat during the day before finalizing our plans to go there.

Regardless of who is doing the itinerary planning, choose locations that will work for **everyone**. If only one person is fascinated with Egyptian history and everyone else is totally bored by it, Egypt may not be the best location for the family. Yes, you want to be open minded and have your travel companions do the same, but you don't want a mutiny on your hands either. After you discover a location that is of interest to you, evaluate why it is of interest and then "sell" your fellow travelers on the idea. We often used travel videos from the library as part of our research and marketing campaign. This was especially helpful with the kids where pictures are worth a thousand words.

If you succeed in your sales technique, then you may have a winning location. If no one is buying, you either need to go back and do additional homework on that location or move on to greener pastures. We did not consistently practice this technique when doing our planning and ended up with some locations favored by the planner, but no one else. Where were our checks and balances in the planning process? Obviously hiding, and we paid the price. We spent ten days in Montevideo, Uruguay which nobody liked at all!

What makes a location right for you will depend on what is important to you, which is more than what sights might be of interest. While big cities have more "to do" than smaller towns, we typically found it was smaller towns that captured our hearts. We could get our hands around them and feel a part of them quicker and easier than larger cities. We would run into the same people each day, locals as well as travelers, helping to create a sense of community. There weren't as many sights to see or as many museums to go to, but the flavor of the town always made up for what might be lacking in terms of "tourist" activities. Often it's not what you see or do that makes a place memorable but what you experience while there. The human interest side is typically not covered in guide books; you have to discover those on your own. Many times, the less of a tourist attraction a location was, the more we loved it.

As part of the planning process, we felt special consideration needed to be given to the first location of our trip. While everyone would be fresh, excited and eager for adventure, we also figured that whatever happened there could have a lasting effect on the whole year ahead. For that reason, we thought an "easier" location was the most appropriate for starters. Rushing into a country where there could be huge language barriers, primitive traveling and living conditions or substantial cultural differences was probably not a good idea if we wanted everyone (especially the kids) to be on board to continue for another eleven plus months. For that reason, we picked The Netherlands to start with. While English is not their native tongue, 85% of the Dutch speak it. The country is easy to get around and since it is a westernized country, the traveling and living conditions were easy to adjust to. The biggest cultural adjustment we had to make in The Netherlands was not wearing a bicycle helmet while riding our bikes! It turned out to be the perfect place to start our journey.

Our thoughts that whatever happened at our first stop could have a lasting impact on the trip proved out on our third day in The Netherlands. We took a day trip into Amsterdam. The Van Gogh Museum, was one of the sights on our agenda. Avocet and Siena have never really had any issues with museums, that is, up till now. They hated the Van Gogh Museum saying it was "totally boring." From that point forward, for the rest of the year, any mention of an art museum was not well received. It didn't matter how "famous" the museum was or how "frequented" it was by other tourists. Any visit to an art museum over the months ahead occurred only after a long fought battle. First impressions are crucial, so select wisely!

Special consideration should also be given to the last several locations of your trip, though we only figured that out in retrospect. We assumed by that point in the journey, everyone could handle just about anything, which they can – they just may not want to! At the end of your trip, you may be getting weary. You have seen umpteen museums, churches, markets, etc. and unless something is unique, no one is all that motivated to get up and go to see more of the same. Everyone is feeling preoccupied with home. For all of these reasons, choose your last several locations wisely: places with lots of fun things to do or places with appealing culture or ambiance. Exploring an activity that is new for everyone is a possibility: snorkeling or scuba diving in the Great Barrier Reef, Horse Trekking in the Andes Mountains, skiing in the Alps. Perhaps you can save the best for last so everyone feels excited until the very end.

Once you have decided where you are going, "get into" those locations as much as possible. Read novels that take place in the countries you have chosen. If you are a nonfiction buff, read about their history, culture, or religions. Find a city's English Language newspaper on line and check in every now and then to see what's going on. It's all a way to build additional excitement around the choices you have made.

You Will End Up In Some Interesting Places...

Monday, November 10, 2008
THE MONKEY TEMPLE
Posted by Avocet at 2:30 AM

We had heard about a temple called The Monkey Temple.
When we got here to Jaipur, Rajasthan, in India, we made a
priority to see it. The Monkey Temple's real name is Galat, a
temple built for the Hindu Sun God, but since there are loads
of monkeys there at dusk, it got the silly nickname of The
Monkey Temple. We got a tuk-tuk out there and it was the
most horrible ride we had ever had. We had an older driver,
calm, gentle, a less crazy driver we thought,but we guessed
wrong. Zoom Zoom Zoom, he was the craziest driver we ever
had!!! But back to the Monkey Temple. If you go, it is the
most bizarre site in the world. Okay, first there are the
animals. There are monkeys and cows which are everywhere.
And then there is food. Animals + food = animal poop. And
that's exactly what there is. Monkey poop pellets and cow
pies are not the kind of thing you want to see at a holy site.
Then, the women in their Sarees and Punjabis and the men in
typical western clothing. But they are all barefoot!!! Now
remember those excretions I was telling you about? Bare
feet + poop = a large mess. And they don't even try to not
step in it!!! Now the garbage. There is garbage
EVERYWHERE!!!!!!!!!!!!!!!!!!!!!!! And the cows eat the garbage
too!! Cows + Garbage = a germ breeding ground. I don't even
want to know what those poor cows are picking up!!! And now,
the site itself. The bare foot people that have walked in the
poop and garbage in their pretty Sarees and Punjabis now
start to finish the unsanitary process by going to a large
green-watered pool, also filled with monkey poop and
garbage. The women go up to the pool, light a candle and set

it afloat on a little raft with the candle aboard. Then you go up further and there is another pool, less garbage (but sill green) and the people were swimming in it!!! The ladies and men, fully dressed, would get into the pool, stand up and dunk their heads into the water!!! The younger girls would just dump buckets of the filthy stuff onto their heads. Green water + people in it = germs. And then you go up even further and there is *another* pool and that one has even *less* garbage in it but the monkeys drink out of that pool. It looks like a mosquito breeding ground to me.

So overall:

There are tons of pretty people but they walk through lots of garbage and poop of the monkeys and cows that hang around and the people feed the monkeys and the cows eat the garbage and the people take off their shoes and they swim in the pools that are "ever so clean" and then they set candles afloat, and this is all on a holy site of the Sun God in Hinduism? Do you now understand why the Monkey Temple is the most bizarre site you will ever see or hear about? If you don't, then you have to read this blog, again.

If read quickly, the last paragraph can be quite amusing.

Chapter Six

ACCOMODATIONS: A PLACE TO CALL HOME

When we decided to take this trip, we knew one thing for certain; we didn't want to feel like tourists all the time. We also knew we would get tired of eating in restaurants and that being with each other twenty four hours a day, seven days a week for a whole year would be extremely challenging, especially without an opportunity for some space. Add to those issues the matter of expense. This was not going to be a luxury year; there was a budget to consider. Many countries only offer hotel rooms for two people so we would have to get two rooms. And eating in restaurants can be costly. Roll all this together and you get one solution – apartments!

Apartments

Once we started seriously looking into apartments, it was a no brainer. An apartment gave us space: not just a private bedroom for Mom and Dad but also living space, separate from bedrooms. When you felt the need for distance from someone, you had somewhere to go. Also, Marty and I are not the best sleepers. I remember vacations where one of us sat in the bathroom reading in the middle of the night to avoid waking the other. Not a problem here, just go into the other room.

Apartments also had kitchens - sometimes large, sometimes small, but a kitchen none the less. They came stocked with the necessities: dishes, glassware, cutlery, pots, pans, cooking utensils. While some were better stocked than others, all allowed us something we wouldn't have been able to do in a hotel or guest house – cook! "What's so great about cooking?" you ask. Eat out in a restaurant enough times in a row and you'll see what's so great about cooking. Look at the prices in the supermarket vs. the prices in a restaurant and you'll see what's so great about cooking. Besides, cooking is a way to not be a tourist, to further experience the culture of a country. There is nothing more cultural than shopping in a local outdoor market and buying food to cook versus being the curious tourist who buys a piece of fruit or snack food. Even supermarkets are a cultural experience, new foods to explore, new behaviors to observe. You get to make fun mistakes like buying pudding instead of yogurt since it's written in Dutch or trying local treats like Manyar (a caramel spread) in Chile.

Whenever we stayed in apartments, we had a ritual. Upon arrival, we would explore our new abode, unpack, settle in and then go to the grocery store to stock up. If it was a late arrival, maybe the trip to the market was for only water, milk and bread for the next morning, followed by a full shopping the next day. It was all part of nesting which made our accommodation far more than a place to lay our heads – it made it our home. At the end of a busy day, we never said "Let's go back to the hotel," we said, "Let's go home." We didn't feel like tourists, we felt like we were living, for a short while, in a foreign country.

Our apartments varied considerably. In Venice, our apartment was a tiny one bedroom, with a pull out couch in the living room/kitchen area. It was, however, on a canal where we could watch the gondolas go by. Since we were there for only four nights, it was acceptable. At the other end of the spectrum, our "apartments" in Haarlem, The Netherlands and Rotorua, New Zealand were not apartments at all, but houses: three bedroom houses that were huge, with beautiful outdoor areas to enjoy. The amenities from apartment to apartment were different, but almost all included an Internet hook-up and washing machine, both exceptionally convenient to have. Other possible amenities included: TV, DVD player, DVD library, telephone, cell phone, CD player, radio, computer, air conditioning, heat, an outdoor area such as a patio, terrace or balcony, bikes and books.

These awesome accommodations were often at a cost LESS than the cost of a hotel in the same city. And that doesn't take into consideration the cost savings incurred by cooking our own meals. As an example, our house in Haarlem, The Netherlands cost $500E per week. Even at the terrible exchange rate at the time, that came to $750 US per week, or just $107 US per night. And that's in an expensive country. I couldn't find even one hotel room at that rate in Holland, let alone the two rooms we would have needed. The cost savings in food was equally amazing. One morning in Haarlem as I was walking into town, I stopped to look at a breakfast menu. For a continental breakfast, (coffee, bread, butter & jam) the price was $5E. Times four, times the twenty one days we were there, breakfast alone would have cost us $420E or $630US. Trust me, we didn't spend anywhere near $630 on coffee, bread, butter & jam at the supermarket and bakery!

But it's so much more than about cost savings. It's about a sense of place. You can't find that in a hotel, hostel or guest house. That sense of place can only come from a place you can call home and we were able to call each and everyone of our apartments "home".

How does one go about finding these places? Thanks to modern technology, it's not as difficult as it once was. You methodically search the Internet for any of the following phrases: short term rentals in _____ (fill in the blank with the city and country that you want to search for); vacation rentals in; apartment rentals in; self catering apartments in; self catering accommodations in; vacation rentals in. Depending on the country you are searching in, certain phrases will produce more results than others, but no matter what, you will find a trail to follow. Keep following that trail until you find an apartment that's right for you. Don't give up your search if page one doesn't bring you the results you are looking for. Individual apartment rentals can easily be hidden on page four or five. Our "find" in Haarlem was on the fourth page of a "short-term" vacation accommodation search site.

What that apartment will look like will depend on your needs but here are some things to keep in mind as you search. Pictures speak a thousand words so try to rent from a web site that includes photos. If you are interested in a unit that doesn't have photos, ask the owner to provide you with them. But pictures can also be deceiving. Never let the pictures keep you from asking all the questions you need to ask – even if the answer looks obvious in the picture. We were fooled more than once by pictures! A photograph shot from a certain angle can make a single bed look like a double or a small room look large.

Ask LOTS of questions. If someone has an issue with answering all of your questions, rent from someone else.

Accommodations: A Place to Call Home

Chances are there are lots of units to choose from. Here is a list of questions to begin with. As you explore your options, you may find you have more questions to add to this list:

1. Where is the unit located? How far from town, public transportation, supermarkets, restaurants, sites of interest, etc.? Ask for distance in miles/kilometers and not minutes.
2. How many bedrooms does the unit have? (This is different from how many rooms it has) How many does it sleep? How big is each bed?
3. What appliances does the kitchen have? Stove (hob), oven, refrigerator, coffee maker, toaster, etc.
4. How big is the unit? Most will quote in square meters. One square meter = 10.76 square feet.
5. Does it come with bed linens, towels, kitchen supplies?
6. What other amenities does it have? Washing machine? TV? DVD player? etc.
7. Does it have an Internet connection? Is it cable or wireless? Does it have a computer?
8. What floor is the unit on? If it is a high floor, is there a lift (elevator) or is it a walk up?
9. What are the arrival and departure arrangements?
10. How much is the unit renting for per week? Does this include everything? Taxes? Cleaning? Other fees?
11. Does the rental rate include any cleanings during your stay?
12. Will they offer a discount for a longer term stay?
13. What type of payment will they accept? Cash, check, credit card.
14. Is a deposit necessary? How will the deposit need to be made?
15. Is a security deposit required? When does it have to be made and when and how will you get it back?
16. Do they have any references?

If this seems like a long list, you're right, it is. But it is worth while to ask each and every one of these questions (and more if you have something to add to the list). Nobody likes surprises and if you don't ask the questions, you WILL get surprises. We thought that we were pretty thorough when reviewing accommodations, but over the course of the year, we had our share of surprises. The worst, and most stressful, was when we arrived at our apartment in Krakow, Poland. It was late, about 11:30 PM. The owners were generous enough to meet us there even at this late hour. The second bedroom, and it's bed were smaller than anticipated, so Siena and Avocet were disappointed. But we figured one could sleep on the sofa bed until next week when my mother was going to arrive. My mother! Oh my God! The apartment was a six story walk up with no lift and my mother, who is 78 years old, with arthritis and COPD, was coming to visit with us and STAY with us for a week! She could barely make it up one flight of stairs let alone six. Despite the fact that the apartment had a very informative web site and I had a good correspondence with its owner in English, I never asked and he never mentioned that the apartment was on the sixth floor of a building with no elevator. I didn't sleep at all that night trying to figure out what we were going to do. The next morning I started searching on line for a new apartment. I also sent an email to the owner who owned other rental units in Krakow. Fortunately, the day before my mother's arrival, we moved into another rental apartment owned by our landlord's mother. This second apartment, in fact, was my second choice of apartments in Krakow. In the end everything worked out fine. But all of this stress, aggravation, and upheaval could have been prevented by asking just one question "What floor is the apartment on and is there an elevator?"

I made a note to ask for distances in mileage. Often distances were quoted to us in minutes. In Korcula, Croatia we asked how far the apartment was from town. We were told "The apartment is just 15 minutes from town." When it took us twice as long to walk into town, we realized Croatians must walk a lot faster than Americans. But I assume they measure distance the same way so it's a better way to determine an apartment's true proximity to points of interest.

Since we stayed in locations for long periods of time (up to three weeks), asking for a long term discount saved us thousands of dollars over the course of a year. With less apartment turn over, the owner saves on cleaning costs and doesn't need to find another renter. They often appreciate your longer stay and in return will give you a discount, but typically, only if you ask for it!

It's not uncommon for owners to ask for a rental deposit. That's fair enough. But try to avoid ones where they ask you to pay for your full stay upfront before arrival. If there is a problem with the accommodation, you don't want to be in the weak position of the owner having all of your money. You will most likely be asked to pay for your full stay upon arrival. Take a good look around the apartment before you fork over the bucks — make sure this is what you had in mind or at least something you can live with.

"Checking out" of an apartment can sometimes be tricky. Unlike a hotel, there is no reception desk where you drop off the key when you are ready to leave. Often the key needs to be returned directly to the owner so you must make arrangements prior to your departure. This was never a problem when we were leaving at a respectable time, but when we had flights that left at absurd hours of the morning, sometimes the situation became a little hairy. We would try to arrange the "check out" the night before, but several times that was not acceptable to the owner who insisted on being there when we left. If they didn't mind getting up in the middle of the night, that was fine, but we feared that if they were late, we could miss our flight. Everyone did show up when they were supposed to, but just in case, we always had in mind a plan "B".

Late departures can present a challenge when staying in apartments. If your flight doesn't leave until later in the day, you have the option of paying for an extra night in order to have use of the apartment for your last day, or of being out by 10:00 or 11:00 AM, with six hours to kill in the city with your **baggage!** For us, each of these situations was handled on a case by case basis. If no one was checking in that day, sometimes the owner let us stay past check out time gratis. In Rome, someone was checking into the apartment immediately and we didn't have a flight till midnight. We left our apartment at 11:00 AM and went to the train station. There they had a luggage checkroom where, for a fee, you could leave your bags. We then spent the day touring Rome. After dinner, we returned to the train station, picked up our luggage, and took a cab to the airport. It was a long day but we survived. We didn't have too many of those but you will have to check your itinerary and plan accordingly.

When you book a room at a hotel, you're pretty sure the hotel will be there when you arrive. The same is not true when you are booking an apartment or house from an individual. Each time we switched countries, I had a pit in my stomach as to whether or not the apartment we had booked in that country really existed. What if it was all a scam? What if they have my deposit and this unit doesn't really exist and we have no place to stay. We booked nineteen apartments and houses around the world and I'm thrilled to report that every one of them existed! Every owner showed up! And every deposit was accounted for! I feel awful that we live in such an untrusting world and that these thoughts would even come to mind. And I feel great that each and every time, my negative thoughts were avenged by humanity.

Hotels/Guest Houses

Do the math. If we were gone for a year but only had apartments booked for 2/3 of our trip, we must have stayed somewhere else for 1/3 of our trip. For the four months through Africa, India and Asia, we stayed in hotels or guest houses. It's not that we were looking for variety; it's just that apartments were not readily available in those countries. Fortunately, these were the cheaper countries, so in terms of cost, our expenses were kept low simply due to the nature of their economies.

We found these accommodations in much the same way as our apartments i.e. on the Internet. For these accommodations, however, we were also able to use guide books and travel websites such as TripAdvisor.com. Occasionally we had a family room that slept all four of us, sometimes all in one big room and sometimes in rooms that were divided. Other times we had two separate rooms. When we did have two rooms, it was our comfort level with our surroundings that dictated the sleeping arrangements. For three nights in Delhi, India, Marty slept in one of the rooms with one of the girls while I slept in the other room with the other. But for a week in Mcleodganj, India, Avocet and Siena had their own room while Marty and I had our own. Trust your gut and go with it. Sometimes we would feel comfortable with the kids sleeping on their own, but they did not. After checking in on their feelings about a particular place, if they weren't OK with being on their own, their feelings would prevail.

Accommodations: A Place to Call Home

Of course the opposite was true as well. Sometimes we were less than comfortable with the kids sleeping separately even though they were fine with it. In that case, the parents' decision prevailed.

We tried to choose hotels that had some type of communal living space: a garden, a lounge, a reading room, a terrace. We treated this communal living space as our "living room". We had a place to go to "get away" from each other and even a place to go when we weren't sleeping well during the night. This communal space helped a lot as we transitioned from having larger living quarters to smaller ones.

Choosing a hotel in one of the cheaper countries can be an opportunity to splurge. In India you can stay in a palace. In Thailand, in one of those huts that stand on stilts over the water. It's not that these are dirt cheap accommodations; it's just that for that type of luxury, it's inexpensive relative to other places in the world. If you are looking to treat yourself to something special, this is the time to do it.

It wasn't until we were out of apartments and into hotels and guest houses that we discovered one of the major disadvantages of apartments. In apartments, you are alone and on your own. In guest houses and hotels, you are around other people and other travelers. We started meeting all kinds of people - interesting people, with great stories to tell. We could have conversations with someone other than each other! We knew we had felt a little isolated, desperate for companionship and conversation, but we attributed this to traveling with children. We didn't take into consideration that when staying in an apartment, we weren't coming into contact with others in the same way we would if we had been staying in other accommodations.

Travel accommodations can also offer another benefit, information. When you are in an apartment, you are totally on your own. Staying in a hotel gives you access to a local who can usually speak your language. You can ask questions and obtain an array of data, helpful to even an independent travel.

Hostels

I don't know a lot about hostels. We stayed in only one for one night. It was clean and convenient but pretty bare bones and it wasn't all that cheap. We took an overnight into the Blue

Mountains from Sydney and stayed in the YHA Hostel there. We were told by other travelers that it was very nice one. Hostels have communal spaces so you have an area to "live in" other than your room. Many also have communal kitchens where you can cook and store food. Some have private rooms, family rooms, or dormitory style rooms. Since you typically pay per person in a hostel, if you are traveling with a family, it may not be as cheap as you think. It's certainly not homey. Before you assume that hostels are your only budget option, shop around and look at apartments.

Pros and Cons: Would We Do It That Way Again

We loved our apartments! On our way from China to Australia, Avocet and Siena were dreaming of not having to get dressed in order to go out to eat breakfast, of eating in their pajamas in our "own" kitchen. We couldn't wait to make a home-cooked meal, to not have to eat in a restaurant. And we were anxious to have space other than our bedrooms that we could call our own - space that was not communal where we could lounge in any attire or even no attire.

On the other hand, through our four months in Africa, India and Asia, we met wonderful people, some of whom we met later on during the trip. Several of these people we still communicate with now that we are home. We would not have met these people had we been staying in apartments the whole time.

I think when it comes down to it, "the whole time" are the operative words. We probably ended up with the perfect balance, totally by accident, but the perfect balance none the less. By unanimous vote, we would not have given up any of our apartments. By the same token, we thoroughly enjoyed most of our other accommodations. Our "other accommodations" were in countries where cooking would have been more challenging given the nature of what's available in the markets. So maybe it was by divine providence that we had difficulty finding short term apartments available in these locations.

The right accommodation can really make or break a location. For shorter stays, this isn't as true as it is for longer stays. But when you are out on the road for a while, your accommodation becomes more than just a place to rest your head at night. It's the closest thing you have to home, so choose wisely.

There's No Place Like Home Except...

Saturday, February 28, 2009
A PLACE LIKE HOME
Posted by Marty at 6:15 AM

Being gone for nine months makes you want "a homey place", an abode that makes you feel comfy. Kinda like crawling into a warm sweater on a cold morning. We have had some really cool places to stay this year. We haven't talked about a lot of them because they just aren't as "cool" as the places we visit. The Pearl Palace Hotel in Jaipur, India with its wonderful owner Mr. Singh was great but did it compare to the Taj Mahal. No way. So you haven't heard about the goods and bads of our accommodations. Till now.

We are currently staying at "The White House", a detached house associated with Sandi's Bed and Breakfast in Rotorua, New Zealand. The place is great. Here's a rundown:

The place is huge; maybe as large as the three floored house in Haarlem in The Netherlands. When we book places we generally know the size, usually quoted in square meters, so we have to do the conversion to square feet. I do this. lisa isn't nearly as anal as I am about numbers. Size is often mentioned with places booked through services such as Homelidays or other travel accommodation sites. But, when you go to an individual, you don't get as much: not the pics by room, not the details of internet access, etc. With Sandi we had a few details but not a lot. Not enough at the beginning to know we had a special place.

Everything works: The stove, the windows, the bathroom (sink and shower) and the DVD player was simple enough to figure out, etc., etc. Our place in Coogee, a suburb of Sydney, had blinds that didn't work, screens that fell out of the windows. We have had ovens that we couldn't figure out or never got hot enough. Here we also have a really big refrigerator. In Venice we had one a little bigger than a cooler; same as in Krakow, St. Helens, Dubrovnik, Korcula, Montepulciano. Big kitchen, little frig.

Here at The White House, the girls have their own bedrooms for the FIRST TIME in their lives. Our first night here they separated at ten o'clock, Avocet to one bedroom with a double bed and Siena to one with a queen. We were scared they would be up throughout the night in our room scared because of the change. No way. They really liked having the rooms to themselves. But this blog isn't about Si and Av, it's about this cool place. I go on.

The thing that makes a place great is how it makes you feel. We just left a three bedroom apt in Christchurch that was very spacious and very efficient but its style was minimalist and lacked warmth. Our great place in Montepulciano in Tuscany was picturesque with great views but we didn't feel as good "together" as we do here. The walls have adornments of paintings or wall hangings that are appropriate and match the room. The living room has an alpaca rug. The window treatments match the carpet. The dining room table has a tablecloth that doesn't look like it came from the Salvation Army. The carpet is clean. The beds have comforters that match the colors of the room. The linens are quality. But it also has that unique intangible that just makes you feel good. Kinda like our rooms at home that we have made into our own. Those rooms make us feel good.

Thanks Sandi. Your place makes us feel good.

Chapter Seven

TO PLAN OR NOT TO PLAN?
THAT IS THE QUESTION

Everyone has their own comfort level when it comes to planning. Some choose to map out a route of where they are going, complete with mileage, time tables and a detailed itinerary of what they are going to do every second of the day. Others are spontaneous, jumping into the car and figuring it out along the way. Most people are somewhere in between. Regardless of where you fall in the planning spectrum, a certain amount of planning is necessary when you are taking a trip of this magnitude. How much planning will depend on a lot of variables:

> Your personality and temperament
> The personalities and temperaments of those traveling with you
> Traveling with or without children
> How you want to spend your travel time
> Type of accommodation you plan to stay in
> Your time and/or desire to plan before leaving

Your Personality and Temperament

I'm a person who likes to feel in control. I Google Map a destination prior to setting out in my car. I call the museum to find out their opening and closing hours and what exhibits are currently being held. And while I can be spontaneous at times and cope with surprises (good and bad) when they happen, overall, that is not my comfort zone. I much prefer having life mapped out as much as possible before I venture out.

So, you have to ask yourself, "What is my comfort zone?" Am I willing to arrive in Amsterdam at 5:00 PM with no previously booked accommodation? Will I freak out if I can't figure out how to get from the Bangkok train station to the Bangkok airport and can't find someone who speaks English? Will I feel burdened dragging my luggage around the streets of Dubrovnik if I don't have a map and or don't know where I am going? When you answer these questions, it is imperative you be honest with yourself or the costs could be high.

The Personalities and Temperament of Those Traveling With You

Marty is much more spontaneous than I. But he likes the comfort of advanced planning when traveling. It is not always the case, however, that you and your travel partner need the same level of advanced planning. In that case, you will have to discuss and decide before hand to what extent you are going to pre-plan your journey. If you have trouble finding a happy medium, I recommend you lean to the side of planning more in advance than not. There will be lots of opportunities for spontaneity and last minute planning (whether you like it or not). Before you leave, however, it is important that everyone feel comfortable with what lies ahead. If the spontaneous person is excited and the planning person is filled with anxiety, it's not going to work.

Traveling With or Without Children

Most adults have the ability to cope with uncertainty better than children do, especially if they are young. So picture this scenario. You have just told your children you are going to be traveling for the next twelve months. They will be leaving their home, their school, their friends, their personal belongings, their routine and everything they have come to know as familiar, for a year of nothing familiar other than their parents. You arrive in Ljubljana, Slovenia. It's a lovely city but you have no idea where you are, where the tourist office is or where you are going to be spending the night. Are your children:

a. Excited by the prospect of roaming around the lovely streets of Ljubljana looking for a hotel?

b. Fearful they will be spending the night on the street with their backpacks as their pillow?

c. Angry that you dragged them on this wild goose chase of a trip that was your gig and not theirs?

For us, the answer to that question was easy. It would have been b & c. Siena and Avocet would have been very unhappy not knowing where they were sleeping that night and they would have been scared. In addition, I wouldn't have been very happy dragging them from hotel to hotel until we found what we had in mind. When it's just adults traveling, the option of planning less works. But when kids are involved, having more definitive plans will keep stress levels down and comfort levels up – a trade off well worth it.

How You Want to Spend Your Travel Time

While life has a way of just happening, travel does not. If you don't book that flight out of Tanzania, you're not leaving Tanzania – at least not voluntarily! If you don't find the bus that will take you to the Wildlife Park just outside of Hobart, Tasmania, you're not going there. You get my point. You are 100% in control of your travel. You will be planning it one way or another; it's just a question of when and where.

The more you plan in advance, the less you have to do while on the road. The less you plan in advance, well, you can figure that one out yourself. So, do you want to spend your time in Yangshou, China biking the countryside? Or, do you want to spend it in an Internet cafe, booking a flight to Vietnam? Would you prefer exploring the Wats of Luang Prabang, Laos or exploring the streets looking for a place to sleep? Planning will take a lot of time! Therefore you need to decide which time you want to use to do the planning: pre-trip time or trip time itself.

To Plan or Not to Plan? That is the Question

Type of Accommodations

We opted to rent apartments for 2/3 of our trip. You don't just roll into Buenos Aires and say, "Let's go find an apartment to stay in for the next two weeks." While hotels, guest houses, or hostels may be available at the last minute, apartments won't be. There are fewer apartments in any given city than there are hotel rooms and they take more detailed research to uncover. To stay in one will require advanced planning. Seasonal rentals will be even more challenging if they are not booked months ahead. If you want to be spontaneous and flexible – apartments are not for you. Keep in mind, however, that if you have specific hotels, guest houses or hostels you want to stay in, you will also need to make advanced bookings. If you choose the non planning route, you have to be willing to take what is available, having no attachments to any particular accommodation.

Your Time or Desire to Plan

What is your life like now, during the pre-trip phase? Is there time you can squeeze out of your already busy life to plan, or is your plate too full? Even if you desire to fully plan your trip before you go, your ability to do so will dictate whether or not this is possible. If you can't plan the trip as much as you like, you and your travel companions should set your planning priorities. Tackle those at the top of your list first and continue to work from there. If you have the time, but not the desire, you must be comfortable with doing things more spontaneously. Plan only the necessities and then wing the rest.

How We Did It

Based on how I described myself, you can probably guess how the Shusterman/Greenwell family did it – we planned it! We planned it all. Well, not everything, but almost everything. Before leaving the United States for our one year trip, we knew exactly where we were going, which countries, which cities and when. We had all but two airfares booked, all but two accommodations reserved, all visas that were needed in advance obtained... We didn't have our day to day activities planned, but we had a notebook with pages for each city we were visiting with detailed information about each and what there was to do once we got there.

We planned and planned and planned. From the moment we started planning to the date of departure was 2½ years. This included planning for both the trip as well as home during our absence. Planning was not a full time job as Marty continued working full time until ten days prior to our departure and I continued a part time job as well as managed our home life. The last six months prior to leaving, we did cut back on volunteer work but other than that, planning occurred in our "spare time": evenings, weekends, lunch hours.

The Pros and Cons of Planning

We loved Mcleodganj, India. We didn't want to leave and would have liked to stay longer than the week we were there. But we had overnight train tickets back to Delhi, accommodations booked in Jaipur and a scheduled flight out of India. We weren't thrilled with Montevideo, Uruguay, but our apartment was fully paid for and our flight didn't leave for another ten days. Peru and Machu Picchu never made it on our finalized itinerary, but after talking with other travelers in South America, we regretted the elimination. All of these desires for something different and almost nothing we could do about it. When you make plans, there is a lot less room for spontaneity. It's harder to stay longer or leave earlier when you want. Changes or alterations to your itinerary are challenging if not totally impossible. When your trip is "planned out," you lose on these accounts. It doesn't mean you can't make any changes, we certainly made some, but you give up most of your flexibility as a trade off for security.

Because everything is not always as you expect, planning ahead can also mean arriving at accommodations that are less than desirable. While this didn't happen to us often, it did happen twice. When you are standing in the lobby of a hotel, hostel or guest house, you can take a look around and get a feel for the place. You can ask to see the room you are about to rent. When you are booking in advance, it's sight unseen or based on a picture on the Internet which may or may not show a "true" picture of your accommodation. If the booking does not require advance payment, you are no worse off for having made the reservation – you can still easily leave. But when payment is required prior to your arrival, you risk paying for something you might want to walk away from.

For a full year I had a wonderful correspondence, in English, with someone from a guest house in Luang Prabang, Laos. The guest house had mostly great reviews and the pictures on line showed a pleasant looking accommodation. About ten months after booking this guest house, and two months prior to arrival, they requested a full payment via Pay Pal. At the time, I really had no reason to believe we wouldn't love staying at this place and went ahead and made the payment. Upon arrival, the disappointment was on everyone's face. This is not what we had in mind for the next ten days. While it may have been on Marty's and my minds, it was on Siena and Avocet's tongues "We don't want to stay here!" We spent the night, but the next day we went walking through town, checking out other guest houses. We found another guest house everyone was happy with, but the big debate was, do we move even if we can't get all our money back. We decided we would move, taking that risk. In the end, we got all of our money back but it could just as easily have worked out the other way. Fortunately, we didn't have too many requests for full payment prior to arrival.

When you make arrangements before you leave home, you have a greater array of services readily available to you; services that are familiar to you, you know work and are in your language. When you are on the road, you are at the mercy of the services available in that country and/or via the Internet. But just because you used an Internet service from your home, don't assume that same service is equally available to you while on the road. A Pay Pal account that worked fine from our computer at home caused us problems when trying to transact business from Italy. Certain transactions will be viewed as fraudulent when the account is opened in one country but business is conducted from another.

Another problem we encountered was when we were booking our Buenos Aires apartment from Rotorua, New Zealand. None of the apartments in Buenos Aires seemed willing to book a rental more than four months in advance so we had to book this one while on the road. The apartment owner wanted a deposit and wanted it in US Dollars. We went to the Western Union and made the request that the amount needed to be paid in US Dollars. We were told we would need to pay in NZ

Dollars (which required an ATM transaction converting US Dollars to NZ Dollars) which would then be converted to Argentinean pesos and then be converted back to US Dollars. Three foreign currency transactions (losing value at each one) in order to make one deposit. From the comfort of our home, prior to leaving, we were able to make deposits in a foreign currency with only one foreign currency transaction and a lot less time; transactions involving only US Dollars were even simpler.

In exchange for our loss of flexibility and the risks associated with pre-paid expenses, we not only had security, we had time; time to do what we wanted to do in each of the places we visited. Or time to relax. We would meet people in Internet cafes making future travel arrangements while we had only to check emails, post blogs, or upload pictures. A good part of our 2 ½ years of planning would have been done on the road had we not done it before hand. That would have taken a lot of time away from "being" where we were. We met plenty of travelers who were doing it this way and I guess it worked for them, but they all agreed it was very time consuming.

Would We Do It The Same Way Again?

YES! No question in my mind. The amount of time spent tending to day to day planning or looking for those few accommodations not yet booked was huge. We would have lost lots of precious time had we not made so many arrangements in advance, time that could never be recouped. Every moment spent in advance planning was well worth it. Besides, while planning is a lot of work, it is also a lot of fun. For 2 ½ years we had the excitement of building this trip one block at a time. The anticipation created during the planning process was almost palpable.

As for lack of flexibility, yes, there were losses, but oh well. We had a year around the world. We didn't see everything. But we went to a multitude of places and saw a plethora of things. There's always next time for what we missed. Advance plans are not concrete. We switched accommodations, cut out cities, changed flights. Some had a financial cost, others did not. Overall, for us, planning was the way to go.

Plan Ahead if you Want to Stay Here...

Sunday, December 14, 2008
<u>MUT MEE GUEST HOUSE — NONG KHAI, THAILAND</u>
Posted by lisa at 1:45 AM

Typically when one travels, you pick your destination and then you find an accommodation at that destination where you desire to stay. We have followed this "formula" for our entire trip with the exception of this one. We came to Nong Khai because that is where the Mut Mee Guesthouse is located.

When researching Southeast Asia trying to decide where we wanted to go, I came across the website for Mut Mee. I immediately decided I wanted to stay there. There were a couple of things to do in Nong Khai that were of interest, but basically, I wanted to go there so I could stay at Mut Mee. So finally, after a two year wait, here we are.

Mut Mee is not a luxurious place. In fact, it is probably the most rustic place that we have stayed in so far. The rooms are simple and the walls are so thin that we can hear every sound coming from the rooms upstairs and next door. You have to pour water into your toilet in order to create a "flush" and you share your bathroom with tiny ants that seem to like to hang out there. So you ask, "What's so special about this place?" It's about the serenity of a garden on the banks of the Mekong. It's about being in a real Thai town that sees very little in the way of tourists. But mostly it's about the community of people who gather here on their way north into Laos or south into Thailand.

While we planned from the beginning to stay here a week, that is the exception vs. the rule. Most people check in for just a night or two but then seem to never leave. The Irish guy at the table next to us came for a night and 4 days later is still here. The Australian at our breakfast table was leaving for Laos this morning but by 11:00 said, "I guess I'll leave tomorrow." The place is very seductive. The garden tables are perpetually filled with people regardless of the time of day. People are talking, playing cards, reading, eating, drinking, painting... Occasionally people leave to go to see a site in Nong Khai or nearby, (there are a few) but mostly people are just hangin. You talk to everyone and one person's life and travels are as interesting as the next. Many people out there think that our family traveling around the world is an unusual adventure, but here, it's just another adventure, nothing terribly unique, for everyone who passes through here is having an adventure of their own.

Tomorrow we will rent a car and drive 70 km to a historical park that is supposed to be incredible. Yesterday we were at a sculpture park that was amazing. But today, like everybody else, were just a-hangin!

Chapter Eight

EMOTIONAL ROLLER COASTER I

None of the planning up to this point came without emotional baggage. We were excited beyond belief about what we were thinking about and planning to do. But at the same time, we wondered if this was the craziest and most stupid thing we've ever thought about. We were overwhelmed by everything that needed to be taken care of and trying to figure out if there was any possible way it could all get done by our targeted departure date. Was this really going to happen or were we just planning for the biggest letdown of our lives? We were happy, sad and lonely. Oh, and scared. Don't forget scared. In fact, scared got bigger the closer we got. Some days I couldn't figure out if I was more scared that it wouldn't happen or more scared that it would.

A year away is big stuff. If we were going out for a shorter amount of time, maybe the emotional roller coaster would be smaller; more of a kiddie ride than one of those super size roller coasters that teens and some adults like to ride. Marty and I talked about it and discovered we are both going through a lot of the same emotions. When it came to the kids, however, we were selective as to what we shared with them. I wanted the kids to know I was scared so that if they felt scared, they knew it was OK and would be willing to share with me. On the other hand, I wanted them to see two strong and confident adults so they would feel secure as they became more aware of the uncertainty ahead of them.

Another feeling I remember having prior to leaving was special. We were about to do something unique. While we knew people who were doing some really cool things (a year in Paris so the kids could learn French, two years in Chile so their family could experience their Mom's culture…), we were the only ones taking a year and going around the world. People would ask us about it all the time. "How is the planning going?" "What destinations have you chosen?" "Will you be doing this?" "Will you be doing that?" I felt like a celebrity and our whole family was the center of attention for almost a year.

Ready or Not...

Friday, May 16, 2008
<u>ARE YOU READY?</u>
Posted by lisa at 1:54 AM

With only 24 days left before we take off, the question that
everyone asks when I see them is, "Are you ready?" And each
time I pause wondering exactly what that question means.
Does it mean do we have our passports, visas, and airline
tickets? Yes! Does it mean do we have our bags packed? Yes!
Does it mean are we ready for the sticker shock that will
occur when we arrive in The Netherlands and see how little
our US Dollar will buy? Probably not! Or does it mean are we
ready to live our life on the road for a year, have our
worldview permanently changed, or begin an odyssey that will
most likely change who we are for the rest of our lives? Yes
and No! How can you possibly ever be ready for that and yet,
if we weren't prepared for that to happen, would we have
ever planned this trip in the first place?

Chapter Nine

FULLY PREPARED FOR THE ROAD AHEAD

To say we planned is an understatement. You can cover a lot of territory in a 2½ year time frame, and we did. There was a certain amount of research necessary in order to establish our itinerary, but our planning went far beyond that. Why so much planning? We wanted to be prepared: prepared in case of an emergency, for our basic needs and for what each and every country had to offer. We didn't want to miss anything. Early in my travel days I took a trip to Greece. It was very loosely put together.   While I had a wonderful time, upon my return, someone asked me if I had been to a particular sight. I hadn't. Not only had I not been to it, I hadn't even known about it. Immediate disappointment set in and I was determined that wouldn't happen again. If I didn't do something on a trip in the future, it was going to be because I didn't want to and not because I didn't know about it

When planning an event of this magnitude it's important to be organized.   It doesn't do any good to have a wealth of information you can't find. I purchased a portable file box; the kind with a handle you can carry anywhere. Inside I put a supply of manila file folders and a black marker. Every time I started research on a new country, I made a new file for that country. If I came across some other interesting information, say health related, a new file was born for that topic. All of our files were stored in this box. If Marty or I took a file out to work on, by the end of the day, it had better be back in that box!

As we researched each city/country, we aimed to have consistent basic information on that location:

1. Medical Information – Name, address and phone number of doctor/clinic/hospital, preferably one with an English speaking doctor
2. Emergency Information – Police/Ambulance/Tourist Police - numbers to call
3. Consulate Information – Name, address and phone number of nearest US Consulate
4. Tourist Information – Locations of tourist information centers in the city
5. English Language Bookstores – Name, address and phone number
6. Internet Sources – Locations
7. Public Transportation Information – All data applicable
8. Airport Information – Specifics on which airport and transportation available to and from the airport
9. Laundry Facilities – Addresses
10. Bank Information – ATM situation and possible locations
11. Travel Agency – Name and address
12. Post Office – Address
13. Public Toilets – Locations
14. Sights/Activities/Museums/Theaters – What it is, where it is, hours of operation, cost, free days, transportation
15. Markets – Location, times, days of the week
16. Supermarkets or other food stores – Location and hours of operation
17. Restaurants – Locations and type of food
18. Cultural Information – Foods of that region to try, eating hours, banking hours, shopping hours, siesta hours, appropriate clothing for the area, appropriate behavior for the area, tipping rules
19. Accommodation suggestions
20. Bike Rental information – Address
21. Day Trip information – Location, transportation, sights to see

We weren't striving to have a day by day itinerary planned before we arrived in any given country, but we were striving to know as much information about a place as possible before ever crossing the border. This type of information enables you to feel in control and gives you the opportunity to travel with confidence. This research wasn't drudgery. It fueled our passions for the trip.

Our first stop on the trip was Haarlem, The Netherlands, a city fifteen minutes from Amsterdam. I discovered there is a bus that goes directly from Schipol Airport to the bus station in Haarlem. I knew exactly where to pick up the bus once I left the airport, where to buy the strip tickets for the bus, the cost and how long it would take to get from the airport to Haarlem. Several days prior to leaving, I also discovered there was a bus strike in The Netherlands. Now what? Well, I turned to my notes to see I also had information regarding the train system. I knew where in the airport to buy a train ticket, the cost, where I needed to take the train to (first into Amsterdam and then transfer trains to catch one to Haarlem), etc. You get the picture. Never did we have to feel like the "lost or confused" tourist. We were able to proceed with confidence and the kids, therefore, had a great sense of security.

Is having all of this information necessary? Yes and No. Some of this information you hope never to use. Emergency information, consulate information, or medical information is for unexpected situations. But, if one of those unexpected situations arises, you'll be glad you had the information at your fingertips. As for the other information, it isn't required, but sure is handy. You can't always find a tourist information office open when you need it and not all cities have them. Sometimes they have them but they aren't all that helpful. And if you are planning on staying in apartments, your accommodation won't have any resources for you. Travel guides are a great option if you are hitting one or two countries, but if you are going to more, the weight and bulk of the books will make that option prohibitive. We met travelers who would pick up a Lonely Planet guidebook each time they entered a new country. But finding an English copy can be challenging at times and very costly. If you want to be informed, doing the research early and keeping a file is the best way to go.

We didn't rely totally on our pre-trip information, but we used it a lot. We also employed information provided by tourist offices, people running our accommodations (sometimes even in apartments) and information picked up via brochures, local "entertainment type" newspapers or even posters. Talking with other travelers is by far one of the best sources of information.

Fully Prepared for the Road Ahead

Before you leave, talk to everyone you know who has gone to any of the places you are considering. Along the way, use travelers who you meet for the most up to date information. Evaluate the information you gather keeping in mind that everyone is different - what is exciting for one person may be a bit too much for you and what they call boring, you might find relaxing and a culturally enriching experience. Anything and everything and anybody were qualified sources of information. Since we had our computer and Internet access most of the time, we were able to do additional research at our convenience. We used TripAdvisor.com relentlessly, posting specific questions and usually getting responses. There are lots of other traveler supported websites available as well. But without the basic information we encountered during our research phase, we often would not have known what to ask or what information to pursue.

The plan was that after the research phase was over, we would take all of our notes and put them in a soft binder to take on the trip with us. But what if that binder got lost? Months of research, our itinerary information, our accommodation information and reservations would be gone. We felt we would be lost. In order to safeguard the information, we scanned each and every page into the computer and then emailed the pages to ourselves. That way, should the binder get lost or stolen, we needed only to be able to access our email accounts in order to recover the information. Did we ever need to do this? Only once! Marty had his notes from Uruguay loose in the backpack while we were out one day. The notes got left behind at a restaurant when they were taken out to read up on some sightseeing opportunities. It was no big deal since we knew we had access to those notes on line. Once all the countries were scanned, we put them all in the binder which traveled in my safely guarded backpack the entire trip.

I suggest writing down information you don't even expect to use. We don't typically use travel agents, but I always had a travel agent written down for each location we were going to. When we needed to book the ferry from Korcula to Rijeka, Croatia, we knew exactly where to go since I had written down the name and address of the travel agent in town who does that type of booking. Marty had not done the same when he was doing his research on Buenos Aires, so when we desired to book a trip to Iguazu Falls, we had to begin by finding a travel agent.

Doing extensive travel planning helps you learn significant details regarding travel in a particular location: like the need to book overnight compartments on Thai trains early as they fill up or about the rip off cab drivers in Prague. In this research phase you will also learn the cultural do's and don'ts: where public displays of affection are inappropriate, that it's not OK to point your feet at Buddha and that it's illegal to have sex with a native of Laos. Your pre-trip planning will uncover all of these things and more. If you are uninformed in some areas, it could be a surprise or an inconvenience. In other areas, it could be a disaster.

If you don't already have a passport in hand, now is the time to apply for one. While you can obtain a US passport pretty quickly if needed, it's best to allow ample time for a non-rush application. An adult passport is valid for ten years and a child's passport is valid for five, so you have no excuse not to go ahead and get one now if you are planning a trip in the near future. Each person traveling will be required to have their own passport including infants. Check out the website travel.state.gov/passport for additional information. If you already own a passport, make sure the expiration date is at least six months past the date you are due back – a year is probably better. In addition to carrying your passport, you should make a copy of the picture page of your passport and carry that with you separate from your passport.

Your passports should be kept in as safe a place as possible at all times. This means they may not always be with you. On travel days, they can be kept in a money belt or, in our case, a special folder stored in my backpack which was **never** out of my sight. But on non travel days, passports were typically left behind. If we could foresee no reason to carry them, we didn't. When staying in apartments, they continued to stay in their folder in my backpack, hidden in the apartment. In guest houses and hotels, they were often stored in a lock box.

We found it helpful to have the needed visas in our possession prior to leaving. A visa is an authorization issued by a government which allows you admission into their country; it is not a guarantee of admission. Because it is not a guarantee, you will want to make sure you either have a visa in your hand or are sure you can fulfill all of the visa requirements, prior to booking a ticket into that country. This can be particularly tricky since often one of the requirements is to have an onward travel ticket i.e. proof you will be leaving their country within their required time frame for visitors. You can find out this information directly from a particular country's consulate or embassy. Don't trust any other source for information on this topic as only the consulate or embassy is guaranteed to have the most up to date information

If a visa was going to be "readily available" upon entry into a country, we opted to obtain it that way (your pre-trip research will provide that information). This minimized the need to juggle our passports and time frames too much prior to leaving. We obtained visas for Tanzania, Thailand, Laos, and Australia (more of a registration than a visa) in this way and had no problems with any of them. Make sure you have the needed amount of cash (in the correct currency and exact change) upon entering a country for which you are trying to obtain an on the spot visa. Don't assume you will be paying for your visa in the local currency; many times you will need US dollars. Carry some extra passport size photos with you for those countries that require them.

If obtaining a visa in transit meant going to a consulate or embassy and leaving our passports (possibly for multiple days), we opted to obtain that visa while still at home. The consulate or embassy may not be convenient, requiring a detour from your itinerary. You may have to overcome language barriers in working with non-English speaking countries. And, of course, when traveling, no one likes to leave their passport anywhere, for any length of time. When applying for visas in advance, look at the date you will need the visa for and for how long the visa will be valid. Having an outdated visa in your passport is the same as having no visa at all. Sometimes you will need to apply for a type of visa other than what you really need to solve the problem of having to apply for a visa so far in advance. Opting for a one year versus a six month visa or a multiple entry versus a single entry visa may remedy the situation. It may cost more, but how much extra would it cost you in terms of transportation and accommodations to get a visa in transit when you weren't planning on being near the embassy. Keep in mind that when applying for a visa in advance, it could take a little while for you to obtain your returned passport. When applying for multiple visas, allow enough time between visa applications and then enough time to receive it back prior to your departure.

In addition to visas and passports, there are a few other documents you might want to have with you. A copy of your marriage certificate is a good thing to carry especially if you and your spouse have different last names. If you are traveling with children who have a different last name from either of the parents, bring along their birth certificates, in addition to your marriage license. If the children traveling with you are not your biological children, carry a copy of the adoption certificate. And, if your children have a biological parent that is not traveling with you, you need a letter from the other parent, signed and notarized. All of these documents should be kept with your passports.

When important documents are lost or stolen, it could be a problem. Having a backup could save you a headache or two. In addition to any original you are carrying, I suggest you have a digital copy as well. This includes all the documents listed above as well as the picture page of your passport. Scan each document into your computer and email these to yourself as an attachment. Hold them in your email archival file. Should you ever need a copy, access your email account and they will be there. In the unfortunate event you find your passports lost or stolen, report it immediately to the local police and then contact your consulate or embassy bringing with you copies you print out from your digital files.

If we didn't have something booked prior to leaving, we knew how to book it, saving us countless hours of research and stress on the road. It enabled us to take care of "business" in a more leisurely manner and when we had Internet access, rather than in moments of pressure or when we lacked a connection. We had information we never needed and saw a multitude of things that were never in our notes, but, in the end, I wouldn't have done it any other way.

One mistake was our lack of maps. A map of each location prior to arrival would have been very helpful. It need not be a full size map, but a one page photo copy map would at least show you the downtown area of the city without adding too much bulk. Once in town, you can typically pick up a more comprehensive map at the tourist office.

No Preparation Needed to Enjoy...

Thursday, February 19, 2009
SWIMMING WITH DOLPHINS – AWESOME!
Posted by Siena at 5:00 AM

When we first got to New Zealand, I saw a brochure for something that said, "Swimming with Dolphins". It was where you got to swim with the tiniest dolphins on Earth: The Hector Dolphins. They're a little smaller than I am right now, and I am pretty tiny, and just about as wide. Just like a lot of other animals out there, The Hector Dolphin is endangered. There are only about 6000 – 7000 of them left and they're all located off the east coast of New Zealand. I didn't think we'd get to do it, but there we were in Akaroa (a town a little ways outside of Christchurch) standing on the main wharf, with wet suits, booties, and snorkeling gear.

There were only ten people in our group as they don't want too many people in the water with the dolphins. It makes them feel crowded. We took a fairly big catamaran and sailed until we reached the end of the harbour. On the way out there, we saw seabirds called Cormorants and three White Flippered Blue Penguins – the tiniest penguins in the world.

The Hector Dolphin likes murkier waters so we went out to the churned up part. Our guide told us to lookout for a dorsal fin just above the water, but that was very hard because there was a lot of seaweed that could easily pass as dorsal fins.

We finally saw two dolphins. They were playing in the waves that the front of the boat was making. The Hector Dolphin is not only tiny, but cute!!!!!! They really like to play and when we got into the water, our guide told us to make noises with our snorkel under water. It was really exciting!!!!!!! They were swimming really near us and would circle around you! The water was very cold though and so I shivered the whole time. We never got to use the snorkeling gear. Since the water was so murky, you wouldn't be able to see anything! After about five minutes, we got back into the boat and headed around the wide open ocean looking for the tiniest, rarest dolphin in the world. We didn't get to swim with them anymore, but from far away we saw one jump in the air! On the way back, we cruised near the rocks and took a look at the seal colony there. We saw one pup nursing!

Swimming with Dolphins was truly amazing!

Chapter Ten

AND FULLY PREPARED AT HOME

Making sure that the home front was going to be taken care of in our absence was almost as much work as planning the trip itself – just not as interesting or as much fun. How much work will depend on your personal situation i.e. what you own, what you plan to keep and what you will do with it in your absence. But even with a long "To Do" list, being organized and setting dead lines for yourself will go a long way toward maintaining sanity.

Some travelers take care of the life they are leaving by ridding themselves of all their worldly possessions, leaving themselves nothing to keep up with while on the road. This is a viable option for some, however, it's not for everyone. Are you willing to come back to no home? Live in a hotel or with family or friends until you find at least a temporary residence? Start all over in a new apartment or house? That car you are driving may be old, but it's still a car - viable transportation. Do you see yourself laying out money to buy a new (or used) car upon your return? Before divesting yourself of possessions, imagine life upon your return without them. There is no right or wrong way to do this, just the way that is right for you.

I couldn't imagine coming back to the US and starting all over anymore than I could imagine landing in Laos without a place to stay. We wanted a place to land when we arrived home which meant keeping what we owned. I also think it would have been difficult for the kids to not have an image of what home looked like. If we sold our house, when the kids said "We miss home," what picture would they conjure up in their minds? Knowing there was a place to come back to created some stability in our lives during a period when there was little to be had.

The House

If you don't own a house and have always been saddened by that fact, now is your opportunity to rejoice. While there are still plenty of things to do that are not related to the house, there is no question about it, preparing the house was the largest responsibility we had.

Since it was clear to us we didn't want to sell the house, the remaining choices were: leaving it vacant for the year, renting it or finding a house sitter. Our first choice was to rent. This meant there would be someone there all the time that would take care of our house and look after it. It also meant we would have some income to help make our monthly mortgage payment. Since we did not want to leave the house vacant, we thought a house sitter would be our second choice. But as we explored that option, that turned out not to be the case. All the house sitters we spoke to expected not only to pay no rent, but also for us to pay for all their utilities. Since we had no control over how high the heat would be turned up or how many lights would be left on all night, this seemed like a potential financial nightmare. We dismissed this idea and leaving the house vacant became option two.

Our house didn't rent until pretty close to the last minute, so it looked as if option two was going to be it. We prepared for this option while still hoping a renter would come along. If you are going to be leaving your house vacant, by choice or not, you will want to make sure you have a "manager" to oversee the care of your house while you are gone. My recommendation is that this not be a friend doing you a favor, but instead, someone who you pay to take on this responsibility. A friend doing this for a week or two is still your friend. A friend doing this month after month will no longer be your friend but someone who resents you for leaving them with this big responsibility. This person should check the house on a regular basis (inside and out) for anything potentially wrong, as well as immediately after any type of damaging weather. If there is a problem, either this person can choose to fix it themselves, (if they are qualified) or hire a contractor to take care of the problem.

And Fully Prepared at Home

Seasonal maintenance on the house can either be handled by the manager or by others you hire. You will want to make sure you have someone to take care of the following items:

> - Mowing Lawn
> - Weeding and other yard work
> - Watering trees and shrubs
> - Watering house foundation in case of drought
> - Raking leaves
> - Shoveling snow
> - Cleaning out gutters

Install timers on your lights so the house has the appearance, as much as possible, of someone living there.

Your utility situation will depend on the climate in which you live and the type of house you have. If you live in an area that freezes, you will need to look into what you should do in order to avoid frozen pipes. Before we ever finished looking into that issue, we had a discussion with our plumber who strongly advised us not to turn off our heat anyway. Since we live in an old (1890) house, with plaster walls, we were told that the plaster would deteriorate if we were to have extreme fluctuations in temperature in the house. This would prevent us from turning off our heat. The good news - we didn't have to look into draining our pipes (we have hot water heat). The bad news - we would have heat bills to pay even though we were not here enjoying the warmth.

If you plan to leave your house vacant, talk with your property and casualty insurance agent to let him know what you are doing and how to best provide coverage for your house. Insurance companies have issues with coverage on vacant houses and without supplemental coverage, your house will not enjoy the same coverage you are used to. Each insurance company has its own time frame, but a vacant house could be defined as any house that has not been continually lived in for as little as two or three months.

About two weeks prior to our departure, option one became a reality and we rented our house. Not finding a renter up to that point, however, was not from lack of trying. We tried all the traditional (and some not so traditional) ways of renting our house. We had a large, professionally made sign with brochures in our front yard beginning six months prior to leaving. The house was listed on Craigslist.org as well as three national home rental sites and we told everyone we knew our situation and to please refer any potential parties to us. Since we live within walking distance of the University of Cincinnati, we sent out a letter to every department head hoping a visiting professor might want to take advantage of living in our house. We also live within walking distance of Hebrew Union College and had a posting there as well. It was word of mouth that finally did it and a local family rented our house. If you are planning on renting, use all the avenues you can think of – you never know where a renter will come from.

Before you put the house up for rent, you will have to figure out under what conditions you want to rent it. Living in an old house with nice hardwood floors, we didn't want to put more wear and tear on them than necessary. We therefore put our house up for rent fully furnished, thereby keeping furniture moves to a minimum. All our furniture would stay put and no new furniture would be moved into the house. We then left it up to the renter as to what personal property they would want left for their use: dishes, pots and pans, bath linens, bed linens, etc. Everything else got packed up and stored.

If your house is rented, you still need a property manager. Your renters will want to have someone to call when something is not working. It's also still a good idea to have someone check on the house's condition, both from natural causes as well as from "renter's causes". Your renter may take over the seasonal responsibilities or you may need to hire out those tasks depending on the rental agreement reached.

Before our renters signed a contract, we presented them with a listing of "Rules and Regulations for the House" which outlined details about how we would like the house taken care of, as well as quirks about our old home they would need to know. We wanted to make sure they had agreed to follow these rules prior to the signing of any agreement. At the time of signing, we obtained one month's rent and a security deposit. We arranged for all future monthly rental payments to be made by automatic deposit directly from their account to ours. To be sure that the electronic fund transfer would work, we requested a $1.00 sample transaction prior to our departure.

Cars

We chose to maintain ownership of both of our cars as we felt selling and repurchasing cars would be more of a hassle than we desired. We have a detached two car garage which we assumed would rent with the house and figured we would have to rent off site storage for our cars for while we were gone. When the house wasn't renting, we decided to lower the monthly rental on the house excluding the garage as part of the rental. That way, we wouldn't have to pay extra to store our cars. Our cars stayed in their usual home for the full year.

To prepare the cars for a year of sitting, we changed the oil supplemented with an additive that is supposed to help cars that will be sitting unused. We made sure the gas tanks were full and added a fuel modifier that helps keep your engine clean. We cleaned the inside of the car, ridding it of any trash or garbage that might make for a science experiment while we were gone, then washed the outside of the car as well. Avoid washing the inside so you don't end up with mildewed carpets. Marty gave a set of keys and the garage door opener to a friend who promised he would stop by at least once a month to start the engines and drive them around the driveway. We left the cars in a backed in position so if at any point the batteries needed to be jumped, the car would be in a good position to do so.

Lastly we contacted our auto insurance agent to adjust the coverage on the vehicles. It's unnecessary to pay liability coverage (the most expensive type of coverage) on cars that won't be driven. We were able to save a lot of money making the proper insurance adjustments for cars that were just sitting there and looking pretty.

Mail

This is a biggie. Assign the job of mail guardian to your most trusted sibling or friend and then promise them a nice present from some remote land of their choice.

Before leaving, convert as many things as possible to "paper free." Companies love this. They get to save hundreds of thousands of dollars by not using paper, printer cartridges, envelopes, postage and labor. You, on the other hand, get to reduce your mail. And while this may not be that important to you, it will be very important to your mail guardian. The less mail they have to deal with, the better! Start winding down magazine subscriptions as well. Don't renew things you aren't going to get a chance to read unless it just so happens to be the favorite publication of your newly appointed mail guardian.

About a month prior to leaving, submit on line a mail forwarding request. As of now, you can only request a six month forwarding notice so you will have to renew it while on the road if you are going to be away longer. Request that the forwarding begin several days prior to your departure. This way you can be sure that the forwarding has actually gone into effect.

Initially there will be a lot of mail. But, if you arranged to go paperless, and you converted all your ongoing bills to on line notification, soon the mail volume will decrease. My sister said that after a month or two, it was as if we hardly existed any more. Nice to know, huh?

What makes this job so important is that the job requires someone else to open your mail to see what, if anything, might need tending to – and you never know what is going to arrive in the mail addressed to you. This person will most likely see personal information including financial data. They will also have to determine how to move forward with anything that shows up and requires some action. They don't have to do it totally alone; you will be available via email. Still, they will need to be trustworthy and dependable or who knows what messes you might have to deal with upon your return.

Taxes

The government has this thing about wanting you to file tax returns here in the US even if you're out trying to prop up another government's economy. They're funny that way. You, as the traveler, have one of two options: The easiest option is to go to the local Internet café and, at the appropriate time, print off forms to file your federal extension from abroad (irs.gov/formspubs/index.html). You can file these forms from wherever you are and then file your returns when you get home. The other option is to hire someone back home to do this. This requires you to gather as much information as possible prior to leaving, (when you are already busy with 50,000 other things) as well as to have your tax preparer coordinate with your mail guardian to supply all the additional information that arrives in the mail. Now you have to pay your tax preparer and buy an extra big gift for your mail guardian who is doing even more work. You and your tax preparer will also have to figure out how you want to handle the issue of signing your tax return since you won't be around to do so.

If you are planning to file an extension, in addition to filing a form, you will need to pay any taxes owed the government for that year. They really aren't interested in waiting until you return home, they want their money now. Again you have two options: write a check (be sure to bring your checkbook along with a minimum number of checks) for an estimated sum of what you might owe for the year, erring on the side of too much in order to avoid a tax penalty, or you can send in an estimated payment before you leave to cover yourselves. We opted for the later. Yes, they have your money for an extra ___ (fill in the blank) months, but you won't have the hassle later.

Prior to leaving, you should check out the rules for your local and state governments concerning extensions. For lots of jurisdictions, filing a federal extension alone is sufficient. But that is not always the case. If there are any extra forms to file, verify you can obtain those on line and if not, secure several copies of each form and keep them in a safe place until needed.

Investments

If you have any investments left after allocating funds for your trip, make sure they are going to be well taken care of. If you have a financial advisor, you are pretty well set. You will want to let her know what you are doing, how to contact you, and ask if you need to sign anything before leaving. After that, it's someone else's problem.

If you are the independent type, however, and don't have anyone watching your nest egg, you will want to be as prepared as possible. With computers and the Internet, it's all very easy. If you haven't already done so, set up your accounts so that everything can be done electronically. You will want to be able to buy, sell and transfer funds on line as well as be able to transfer money to another account. All statements should be paperless and you should have an international contact number of someone who you can call if necessary.

If you have been an active trader up till now, this might be the time for a change. Do you want to be in Yangshou, China worrying about a particular stock or bond? Or searching for an Internet café in Venice because now is the time to sell that utility stock or to buy that manufacturing company? It will be tough to be present with your travels if you are still trying to manage a stock and bond portfolio back home. Set up your investments in long term buy and hold positions and then relax. Once you return home, you can go back to your old style of investing if you desire. Or, you might like the ease of the new style and chose to stick with it.

Voting

If you will be gone during an election and voting is important to you, you need to plan ahead. Maybe it's just a small election and you don't care if you get to vote. Or maybe you're OK with either of the candidates, so it's no big thing either way. We were going to be gone during the presidential election of 2008 and we wanted to have our votes count.

By the time you make your trip, possibly they will have absentee computer voting which would make life a lot easier. As of now, absentee voting is done by paper. You submit a request for an absentee ballot in writing. On that request, you will need to put an address where they can mail your absentee ballot. If you're on the go, this aspect becomes a little challenging. You have to guesstimate where you will be at the time they begin mailing absentee ballots, allowing for mailing time. Then, as if that isn't challenging enough, you have to have a mailing address for that location.

At the time of the 2008 presidential election we were to be in Jaipur, India. But at the time during which absentee ballots would be mailed out, we would be in Zanzibar, Tanzania. Since we were staying at a guest house in Zanzibar, we gave the address of our guest house and sent an email to the guest house owner to be on the look out for two pieces of mail coming their way addressed to Marty and me. We had to guess which day the US Government was going to mail absentee ballots, how long it would take to get to Africa, pinpoint the week that we would be in Zanzibar, and lastly, depend on the Tanzanian postal system to get the mail to us in Zanzibar. This sounded like a disaster waiting to happen!

I made numerous calls to find out how we could still vote if our absentee ballots never showed up. It turns out there is an emergency absentee ballot. You must still apply for an absentee ballot, but if you never receive it, you can use this emergency absentee ballot form. We carried these two forms, along with addressed envelopes, in our important papers. Needless to say, no absentee ballots ever arrived at the Clove Hotel in Zanzibar. We used our emergency absentee ballots, kissed the envelopes goodbye, and hoped that the system worked better in reverse.

On November 4, 2008, we were staying in the lovely Pearl Palace Hotel in Jaipur. While the name may conjure up luxury, we are talking about a two star hotel that cost us all of $16.00 US per night. We had a TV in the room but we had no way of obtaining a channel that would broadcast the election results in English. We asked the hotel owner, Mr. Singh, if there was anyplace close by that would be open early in the morning (Rajasthan is 12 ½ hours ahead of Pacific Time) where we could watch election results. He said he would look into it. Upon returning to our room after a day of sightseeing, we walked in to discover that in our absence, Mr. Singh had a cable box installed on our TV. We could watch election results in the comfort of our own room due to the wonderful hospitality of our hotelier; thank you Mr. Singh!

Health Insurance

Nobody wants to think about getting sick, let alone while being away from home, but you must be realistic. The good news is, international health insurance is not that expensive due to its short term nature and the affordable cost of health care outside of the United States. Through Multiwriters International, we were able to obtain an international health insurance policy, with a $1000 deductible, that covered all four of us for less than $2000 for the whole year. That's only $167 per month for the peace of mind of knowing that if something serious went wrong, we could be cared for, air lifted to a more appropriate health center for treatment, flown home in case of a death and reimbursed for expenses if our trip was interrupted due to a serious illness. I certainly wouldn't leave home without this insurance. While we opted for the Multiwriters International policy, most of the policies I looked at offered about the same coverage for about the same price. Some polices offer more comprehensive coverage (for a corresponding increase in price), but for the value and what we felt we needed in terms of coverage, this seemed more than sufficient.

One problem with an international health insurance policy is just that, it's an international policy - not valid for any coverage once you're on American soil. What happens if you develop a serious illness and want to come home to be treated? You have coverage that will get you here, but none that will pay for treatment you once you do so. If something happens to you on the trip which does not force you to come home, but does have a permanent effect on your health, will you be able to obtain new domestic health coverage upon your return? And what about the rule we have here in the US that for pre-existing conditions to be covered under a policy, we had to have had continuous coverage of health insurance? Will they see the international policy as having had continuous coverage?

Since we had to quit all employment in order to take this trip, there was no longer any group health insurance coverage we could turn to. So, in addition to the international policy, we opted to obtain an individual, high deductible, catastrophic, domestic health plan. Unfortunately, even though we had no intention of using this plan during the year we were gone, this catastrophic plan cost almost double that of the more comprehensive international plan we had obtained. But we had peace of mind. We knew that even under the worse case scenario, we were protecting our health and not leaving ourselves exposed to financial ruin.

Travel Registration

If an emergency occurred, a natural disaster or political unrest in a country where you are traveling, the US Government is willing to help, provided they know where to find you. The only way they can find you is if you register your trip. Go online to travel.state.gov and you will find a lot of information about traveling abroad that is worth your perusal. In addition, you have the opportunity to click on "Registration with Embassies" where you will be able to register your trip's itinerary. This way, you are recorded as an American abroad and the US Government has the ability to locate you if necessary.

Thursday, October 9, 2008
JAMBO TANZANIA
Posted by Siena at 3:00 AM

Jambo everybody, welcome to Tanzania!! My name is Siena and I will be your guide through your on line trip to Tanzania. Before we go anywhere, let me tell you a little bit about Tanzania. The first thing you need to know is that everyone here is black. Black, black, black. Not that that's a bad thing, it's just that it's a little uncomfortable not seeing hardly any white people, except in hotels. Then you see all white people.

The souvenirs here are not those corny snow globes or key chains, just get a wood carving! Tanzania (and other parts of Africa) is famous for their wood carvings, drums, artwork, dancing, and bead work.

Tanzania has no shortage of bananas. Here they have fruit bananas, cooking bananas and beer bananas (yes you can make beer out of bananas), and a lot more. Sometimes you will see trucks or bikes piled high with bananas. You may also see women or girls carrying baskets of bananas on their heads. They learn to do this at an early age. Other foods they eat here are ugali (a food made of corn powder that you eat with your hands and has the texture of a mashed potato), and rice. There is also a lot of Indian food here.

There are over 120 tribes that make up the citizens of Tanzania who co-exist in peace. Other tribes have chosen not to intermix but to stay separate. Each tribe has its own language, and some of the words are still used today. We will use the Masai tribe for an example. The Masai are famous

for their bead work necklaces and bracelets. Some Masai
words are still used for other countries in Africa. Here are
the countries.

Ethiopia – moon
Egypt – where are you going?
Kenya – end of the road

Well, before you go off and explore Tanzania all by yourself,
let me give you a short Swahili lesson:

tembo – elephant
asante – thank you
sana – very much
bas – enough
jambo – hello
pole pole – go slow
rafiki – friends
simba – lion
mama – woman
hakuna matata – no worries
tiki tiki mto – watermelon
karibu – welcome

Asante Sana! We hope you come again.

Chapter Eleven

24/7 FOR HOW MANY DAYS?

Now that you've decided to take this trip, reality is setting in. You will be with your spouse, partner and/or kids for 24 hours a day, 7 days a week, for how many days? 90? 180? 365? Is this possible? After a three week vacation, aren't we all ready to get back to our "normal life" without having our loved ones attached to us by an umbilical cord? What makes us think we can make this trip and not end up on the post office wall as one of the Ten Most Wanted?

The first thing to remember is that wherever you go, there you are. In other words, just because you're changing your venue, it doesn't mean anything else about you is changing, you are just taking it with you. The same applies to your spouse, partner and kids. If there are issues between you and your partner, they will come on the road with you – free of charge! You don't even have to buy a plane ticket for them. Your hormonal daughter will still be hormonal in China (maybe more so) and your irresponsible son will still be irresponsible in Argentina. Long term travel is not one of those things that will "fix" your "falling apart" family or your wounded marriage. Yes, it will be an incredible bonding experience, but it won't be easy, and if you are already experiencing problems, this will only serve to magnify them.

That said, don't take any of this to imply that we have a pristine marriage. We had our fair share of issues, but we had no delusion (at least I didn't) that this was going to be a cakewalk. We were not thinking that "having a baby" was going to improve our marriage in anyway and were well aware that this "baby" could truly make things worse. And it did! The constancy of being with each other all the time, the dependency created by traveling together, the lack of time to yourself, the stress of many new and different situations, all added up to some challenging situations. You know how all those cute, endearing qualities of your spouse when you first met are now sources of irritation? Well, when traveling together, that irritation never goes away. It never goes to work for the day, or out for an evening with friends – it's always there!

As for your children…they too are always there! They are not going to school or having a sleepover with their friends. They are not going to summer camp or to the movies. If they are young like ours are, they are not even going to be left alone while you go out to dinner with your partner. You are going to be with them ALL THE TIME! Which means, you are going to be a parent ALL THE TIME! No matter how much you love your children, everyone looks forward to a break from them. Absence makes the heart grow fonder right? Well, there is no absence here.

Now that I have painted such a "rosy" picture of long term travel, why exactly would you want to go? Because you will be creating life time memories for yourself and your family. You will forever have this experience to bond you. As Bogie says, "You will always have Paris"! Picture yourselves sitting around the dinner table one night talking about that horse trek in the dunes of Chile or being in Thailand when the government was overthrown and the airport was shut down. For all these reasons, you will find some way to cope with these different personalities for your time together.

First you need to figure out how to create some space - space for yourself as an individual and space for yourselves as a couple. Physical space can help generate emotional space and our use of apartments was key to this factor. Apartments gave us marital space – a separate bedroom for the parents. We have a separate bedroom from our children at home, why not on the road? If you are traveling for two weeks, you can deal with all sharing a hotel room, but for fifty two weeks? Aside from the obvious reasons for wanting a separate bedroom, it also gives you an opportunity to just be away from your children: to talk, to read, to be adults and not parents. Apartments also gave us a living space separate from our bedrooms. Having a separate living space enabled us to be alone sometimes, creating an opportunity to do whatever it is you want to do without disturbing someone else.

Something we talked about prior to going but were poor at implementing was separating during the day. We bought two cameras thinking there would be times when Marty and Avocet would be in one place while Siena and I would be elsewhere. Or that Marty would have both kids while I had time to myself. We did do this, but not nearly enough. If there was something Marty really wanted to do, like go to the Maritime Museum in Auckland, and no one else was interested, he went and did it by himself. Or there was the time that I wanted to visit the Holocaust Museum in Buenos Aires and went by myself. Creating more of these opportunities might have helped diffuse some of the stress associated with being together so much. But the majority of our separations were short term: grocery shopping, running to pick up tickets at the train station, a visit to the acupuncturist. This was also true of separations of the kids. Maybe I would go to the bakery with Avocet while Siena stayed home with Marty. But in terms of any bigger activity, the kids were always together with at least one parent, but typically with both.

Why were these separations something we thought about doing, wanted to do, knew we should do, but didn't? I believe it's because no one wanted to give up on doing something as a family. One day I went to lunch with a friend I was visiting in Auckland, while Marty and the girls went to a museum. Since I really wanted to have some girl time, I didn't think too much about the museum I was going to miss, especially since it was MOTAT, the Museum of Transportation and Technology. When the girls came home all excited about the really cool Undercover Spy exhibit they had visited, I felt as if I missed something – not just the exhibit, but the family experience. The problem wasn't going out and doing something by yourself, the problem was what everyone else was going to be doing in your absence. We never really got over this one and in all honesty, I think it would have served us well to have successfully created more opportunities for separation.

Getting along on the road, just like at home, requires good communication. This is needed even more on the road because the types of things you are communicating about are so different from your previous day to day communications, that without clarity, no one really knows what you are talking about. There needs to be continuous open discussion about everything. Once a week family (or couple) meetings are a great idea to talk about what's working, what's not and what's coming up on the agenda. Everyone should get to participate in the discussion and have a say. Children will need to understand that while everyone may get a vote, sometimes their vote doesn't count quite as much as the adult vote due to safety or practical reasons. On the other hand, sometimes their vote may count more. Either way, we always encouraged full participation in discussions.

We did an incredible amount of planning prior to taking this trip, but one area not well planned, that would also have served us well, was to work out our responsibilities i.e. who is in charge of what. I guess I was just hoping we would fall into a nice flow where everyone just pitched in and helped out and everything would get done. WRONG! It's a nice thought, idyllic even, but don't count on it. If there is one person in your family who tends to be the proactive person, that role will cross the Atlantic with them. If there is a decision maker, he/she too will keep that role – unless you decide otherwise. Planning out responsibilities in advance takes the pressure off of wondering who is going to do what.

If you are going to be homeschooling, decide who is in charge of what subjects and when they are going to be taught. Who is going to be doing the food shopping, the cooking, the cleaning, the day to day sightseeing planning, etc? It's worth taking extra time to sort this out from the beginning – it may just keep you from killing each other.

Some Days, Life Looks Like This...

Tuesday, December 30, 2008
THE CYCLE OF TALKING
Posted by Siena at 2:21 AM

When we started our trip it was easier to get along with each other. Now, six and a half months out, we crane our heads over the crowd to look for people to talk to other than each other. That's okay, it works!! The only problem is, when we can't find someone that's open to talk to, it results in.......................constantly being bored with each other.

Every morning, I wake up and see Avocet sleeping in the same bed or in the bed right next to me. If she's awake, (most of the time she wakes up before me) we play with Seelia and Fuzzy or our dolls. Then Mom and Dad will come in to say good morning. We go out together, talk together, and see each other, **EVERY SINGLE DAY**!!! Seeing each other everyday results in more arguments, annoyance, calling each other names, frustration, etc., etc., etc.,.

Whenever we hear someone speaking English, we POUNCE!! I mean we don't literally, "pounce on them," we just go up to them and start talking. The good thing about this is that we now know a lot more travelers that are doing the same thing as us. The bad thing is that when we have apartments, we go crazy, as there is only our family staying at the apartment and no one to talk to but ourselves and the wall. The whole thing is just one, huge, endless cycle!

Chapter Twelve

WHAT ABOUT SCHOOL???

If you are about to take this long trip with children, high on the FAQ list will be "What about school?" I found this to be a pretty strange question. To paraphrase Mark Twain, "Why let school get in the way of a good education." We never doubted that the girls would learn more during this year of travel than in a classroom. Not only would they learn more, but what they learned would be more relevant to their lives than their fourth grade curriculum.

For example: In the state of Ohio, you learn about Ohio history in fourth grade. Now I didn't move to Ohio until I was thirty-four. So, since I grew up in Pennsylvania, I learned Pennsylvania history when I was in fourth grade. Now here I am living in Ohio and no one really seems to care about the Pennsylvania history I learned and I know nothing about the history of Ohio. But on the road, Avocet and Siena learned world geography. They learned there is a country called Slovenia which is different than Slovakia (which appears to be a source of confusion for several of our US presidents) and where they are located. They learned that Tasmania is not a separate country but is a state in Australia. And they learned that New Zealand is considered the gateway to the seventh continent, Antarctica. This information will serve them well regardless of which state (or country) they choose to live in.

Because of state requirements for school, it is probably easier to remove your children for a full year of school than to remove them for just part of the year. If you take them out for just the beginning of the year, they will be required to take the standardized exams for that school year and therefore what you teach them on the road will need to follow the curriculum for the grade they attend. If you are gone for the whole year, you are technically homeschooling them and therefore they won't be required to take the standardized tests for that year. Your curriculum can be oriented to what you are doing and where you are going versus what your school is teaching while you are away.

To say we homeschooled for the year we were gone would be somewhat of a misnomer. More accurately, we non-schooled. We didn't follow a designed (ours or others) curriculum, we didn't sit down each day for X number of hours to teach, we didn't assign homework or research projects; the kids just learned. They learned about whatever it was we were looking at or doing on that particular day. And they learned from the discussions that occurred when their minds were sparked by the things they saw or did.

The only lessons formally taught were math. This is the one area where we felt they needed to keep current with what was being taught at their grade level so they could move to fifth grade without detriment. We obtained some math workbooks that covered the fourth grade curriculum and purchased a computer program with similar subject matter. We didn't work everyday, just on days when it was convenient. If we had a "down day" or a travel day, we usually took advantage of those to do some math. On days where we were busy with "sightseeing," we would pass.

So, if the only subject we formally taught was math, what and how did the kids learn? Both Siena and Avocet are avid readers so they read books, lots of books. They started off with what we brought from home and after that, they read whatever English Language books we could get our hands on. They both kept journals which they wrote in each day (or sometimes every several days, playing catch up) and wrote blog entries regularly. While we never reviewed their journals for privacy reasons, we did review their blog entries with them before they were published, checking spelling, grammar and writing style.

We hadn't prepared a syllabus prior to leaving, but upon our return, the school was looking for some "proof" of having educated our children for the year we were gone. Marty sat down and wrote up this summary of Avocet and Siena's education for the year:

CURRICULUM

Student's name: Avocet Orly Greenwell and Siena Skye Greenwell

School name: Worldview Elementary

School address: The world...From June 10, 2008 until June 3, 2009, the Greenwell/ Shusterman family circumnavigated the globe, visiting forty separate locations in seventeen countries.

Parents: lisa Shusterman, BA in Anthropology from University of North Carolina, Chapel Hill 1981
    Marty Greenwell, BA in Accounting from University of Kentucky, 1976

Brief outline of curriculum:

MATH

Successfully completed the Key to Fractions series, published by Key Curriculum Press (recommended by teachers at North Avondale Montessori). This series consists of:

Book 1: Fraction Concepts
Book 2: Multiplying and Dividing Fractions
Book 3: Adding and Subtracting Fractions
Book 4: Mixed Numbers

Also completed MathMedia, an educational software series on decimals, including: decimal basics, reading from a graph, least to greatest, rounding and estimating, converting decimals to fractions and comparing fractions and decimals.

Percents successfully taught by lisa Shusterman

LANGUAGE ARTS

Avocet and Siena were exposed to languages around the world. They successfully navigated their way through menus and basic communication in the following languages: Dutch, Polish, Croatian, Slovene (also took a two hour course in basic Slovene conducted by the Visitor's Bureau in Ljubljana), Italian, Swahili, Hindi, Thai, Lao, Chinese, and Spanish. Avocet and Siena also successfully completed 32 hours of Spanish language tutoring in Chillan, Chile, Valparaiso, Chile and Buenos Aires, Argentina. Successfully mastered basic communication in Spanish.

READING

Both Siena and Avocet are avid readers. They have successfully read the following novels: all sevens books in the Harry Potter series (before this year), Tears of the Salamander by Peter Dickinson, The Hobitt and Lord of the Rings trilogy by JRR Tolkein, The Diary of Anne Frank, Tales of Ancient Egypt, Arabian Nights, Journey to the Center of the Earth by Jules Verne, City of Masks and City of Stars by Mary Hoffman, The Last Olympian by Rick Riordan, The Mysterious Benedict Society and the Perilous Journey by Trenton Lee Stewart, Caddie Woodlawn, the entire Prelude to Dune series by Brian Herbert and Kevin J. Anderson, Daisy Fay and the Miracle Man by Fannie Flagg. Avocet and Siena have read approximately 100 books each in the past year, most well above their grade level. Each can read an average of 200 pages per day on a "normal" day.

SPELLING

Spelling was reviewed this year by both parents as they wrote their portion of blog posts on our trip around the world.

WRITING

Avocet contributed thirty-six blog posts and Siena contributed thirty-five blog posts to the family blog: Oneworldonetrip.blogspot.com. They have both received critical acclaim for their writing style and have been accused of having their parents write the posts for them. This is not true. They originated their blog post themes, all of which had a successful beginning, middle (body) and conclusion and instilled humor into ones when appropriate.

In addition to the blog posts, the girls were required to keep a personal journal of their thoughts and feelings as the family went from country to country. This was not read by the parents in order to protect their privacy.

GEOGRAPHY

Having spent a year traveling, Avocet and Siena know more geography than almost all adults we know. They experienced first hand the majesty of European churches, the incredible wildlife of Africa, the beauty and poverty of India, the serenity of Southeast Asia, the "European-ness" of Australia and New Zealand, the mystery of Rapa Nui (Easter Island), and the simplicity of three months in South America. They have seen world landmarks such as the Taj Mahal, Iguazu Falls in Argentina, the Leaning Tower of Pisa, all of Rome's ancient sights and the Sydney Opera House. They have been in the presence of His Holiness the Dalai Lama in Mcleodganj, India. The girls were in Thailand when people protesting the government closed Bangkok's airport and forced the president to step down. They were active participants in philosophical discussions on war, communism, poverty, religions, prostitution (yes, even that) and how people treat their fellow people. Having seen conditions in the world, Avocet and Siena gave up their Hanukkah gifts to world charities of their choosing.

SCIENCE

They were exposed to many scientific principles over the past year, many of which gravitated into "projects" to figure out why an event occurred. These exposures included 1) Why the Leaning Tower of Pisa is leaning, 2) Why subway cars don't run into each other in Buenos Aires, 3) Wind power and how it was central to "drying" out olden Holland, 4) Determining what animals have to eat constantly based upon the consistency of their stool, 5) How altitude impacts you and your cooking (determined at 14, 200 feet in Ecuador), 6) How to build simple buildings and have them last (or not last)...India, Thailand, Chile, etc. and so on. We also observed marine life in New Zealand by swimming with Hector Dolphins and observing Sperm Whales. A full day was spent at the International Antarctic Center in Christchurch, New Zealand.

After Marty completed this syllabus, we both sat there looking at this document in amazement. Not only for all of the things listed that the girls learned, but for all the things that they learned that were not even included in this document! We knew it was an educational year; we just hadn't put it down on paper and seen it quite that way before.

In our opinion, the greatest amount of learning took place during dinner. The girls would absorb the things we did or saw during the day and then ask the most provocative questions at dinner. This is what Marty was alluding to when he wrote on the syllabus "They were active participants in philosophical discussions on war, communism, poverty, religions, prostitution (yes, even that) and how people treat their fellow people." They would see Lao UXO and wonder what it meant. Explaining the Unexploded Ordnance Program led to a discussion of not only what unexploded land mines are, but why they are there, and what the Vietnam War (called the American War in Southeast Asia) was about and how it got started. Seeing lots of older western men with younger Thai women raised questions and led to discussions about prostitution. Not being able to get onto certain web sites in China raised questions about censorship. Neither Marty nor I were prepared for the sophistication of the dinner table conversations and some nights I would just have to say, "Let's table that conversation for another time, I don't have the energy for a conversation like this right now."

Before leaving home, check with your school both at the local and state levels to find out what will be required upon your return so your child can advance to the next grade level. With the education they are going to be getting, there is no reason they should have to repeat a grade. I recommend that if at all possible, you obtain these requirements in writing. I was originally told that nothing would be needed if we were out of the country, but then, upon our return, they wanted "proof" of a fourth grade education.

Would Your Kids Rather Learn This?...

Monday, January 26, 2009
<u>KOALA PARK SANCTUARY</u>
Posted by Avocet at 6:00 AM

I (the miraculous me) had been planning a day in Sydney. Siena and I had showed much interest in seeing koalas, kangaroos, wallabies, kookaburras and so on. So, when I was planning my day, I started looking at all the possible animal options, and here in New South Wales, they are endless. Finally, the Koala Park Sanctuary was picked.

We went out there on a Monday. Siena and I had packed a picnic lunch in case there wasn't a restaurant on the premises. We left very early in the morning, 7:20 to be exact, as we had to take a bus, a train, and yet another bus to get there. We finally arrived at 9:30, enough time to see all the animals desired and all the presentations the park had to offer. We first headed toward the koalas, the park's main attraction. During the koala presentation, we learned that koalas are extremely lazy, 18 to 19 hours a day are used for sleeping!!! The rest are for eating. They only eat eucalyptus leaves, also known as gum leaves. The eucalyptus gives them enough hydration without their having to drink water. But the leaves are also hard on their digestive system which by the way is 4 meters long!

Next we saw a man sheering sheep and throwing boomerangs. The sheep looked very desperate to get away from the man and away from the sheep dogs too. When the man threw the boomerang, it accidentally got stuck in a tree and that was the end of the presentation.

100

Next, the famous wombat. We got to touch them. Surprisingly they are not as soft as they appear to be. Instead they are very coarse, most likely a trait needed for their borrowing lifestyle. Wombats, like kangaroos, are marsupials. Their pouches, however, are backwards!!! This is because when they dig, they don't want their babies to get dirt in their eyes. The wombats are actually distant cousins of koalas!!!

And for the last presentation, the fairy penguins. They are small, sleek and shy. We didn't see them at first, but when the food came, they thought it was irresistible and had to come out. You can see them in Sydney and Darling Harbor, you just might have to strain your eyes as they are very small.

Next, we bought food (honey nut cheerios) and went to feed the gray kangaroos. They are extremely cute, especially the joeys! We saw one mama with a joey in her pouch, but the head wasn't sticking out, the legs were!!! There were also two joeys outside a pouch, with dad. When I tried to feed them, the dad would nudge their heads aside and take the food for himself!!! What a food hog!

We left the park at about 2:30 to go back to Coogee. It was a long way there and back but we had a very fun day!!!!

Chapter Thirteen

IN SICKNESS AND IN HEALTH

Health is a big issue. Certainly, if you didn't have your health, you wouldn't be thinking about taking a long term trip. And, if you don't keep your health, you won't be able to continue your trip once you've started. While your health is not always in your hands, there are lots of things you can do to minimize the risks.

Immunizations

Having proper and up to date vaccinations is the first step to insuring a healthy trip. A visit to the CDC (Center for Disease Control) website will give you a good idea as to what immunizations and health precautions are necessary for the countries you are planning to visit. If you are willing to go anywhere regardless of the health risks involved, I recommend you visit this website after you have set your itinerary so you can check out the specific countries you plan to visit. If, on the other hand, you feel you are unwilling to expose yourself or your family to certain health risks, you should visit this site prior to setting your itinerary so you know which countries to avoid. If you find it unacceptable to get a yellow fever vaccination or don't want to expose yourself to the risk of malaria, it would be pointless to plan to go to one of the countries where these diseases are a risk. You might as well find out before hand which areas are to be eliminated so you don't set your sites on a location only to be later disappointed after a visit to the CDC website.

A travel doctor is an additional way to explore the health advisories for various locations. Many travel doctors will prepare an individualized plan for you based on where you tell them you want to go. This booklet can then be reviewed at home and used for the preparation of your trip. Chances are you will be consulting a travel doctor at some point as they are the ones who make available the less common vaccinations. When scheduling a consultation, ask if the fee for the consultation can later be applied to the actual doctor's visit. Many of them credit you for the consultation fee if you later use their services.

There are three types of immunizations: routine, recommended and required. Routine are those vaccinations you received as a child (or at least were recommended). Some of those require booster shots at certain intervals to keep you protected while others require no additional shots. Recommended immunizations are additional vaccinations the Center for Disease Control recommends for extra protection given the risks inherent in the areas you will be traveling. Required ones are those immunizations which are mandatory for entrance to a country either because you are at risk in that country or you have recently been to a country where you were at risk. At this time, the only required vaccination is yellow fever, needed for many Sub-Saharan African countries and some tropical South American countries.

Look into your health recommendations long before you are planning to leave. This allows time for research, talks with your doctor, family discussion and gives you adequate time to act on your decisions. Since many of these vaccinations require multiple shots, possibly spaced months apart, you will need ample time to receive all of the chosen injections prior to leaving.

Ironically, when our children were born, I chose to not vaccinate them for certain diseases. I felt it was better to let them get some of these childhood diseases and build up their own immunity than to receive the "artificial" immunity provided by a vaccine. By the time Siena and Avocet were nine years old and we were in the throes of planning this trip, they had still not contracted measles, chicken pox or anything else I had "planned" for them to get. While I was willing to have them experience these diseases here in the US under somewhat controlled circumstances, I was not up for a case of chicken pox in Tanzania or measles in Uruguay. At the age of nine, our girls then had to receive a number of the "routine" shots as well as those "recommended." Even as adults, some of the routine shots were needed. Marty at fifty-three had never had chicken pox and when we were younger, there was no such vaccine available.

Other than the required yellow fever vaccination, which immunizations you choose to get are a personal decision. I could still have chosen to leave my children vaccine free for those routine vaccinations as long as no country was making it a requirement. Keep in mind that many diseases which are not prevalent here in the US, exist to a greater degree in other countries. When trying to decide which immunizations to obtain, think about not only which countries you are going to, but where in that country you are traveling and what activities you might be doing once there. Different areas have different risks: low lands vs. mountains, coastal vs. jungle, city vs. rural. Based on our itinerary, the rabies vaccine was recommended. It would have required three shots per person at over $100 per shot. Cost alone should not be a determining factor in your choice, but in our case, we figured most of our days would not be in rural areas or in situations with a high risk exposure. This of course was a big risk we were taking since rabies is a fatal disease. But after careful evaluation, we decided it was a reasonable risk to take.

Whatever immunizations you choose to get, shop around to find the "best buy in town." While travel doctors offer one stop shopping, it may be the most expensive option. We were able to get all our routine and recommended immunizations at the city health clinic at a fraction of the cost quoted by the travel doctor. In the end, we got only the yellow fever shot from the travel doctor. Check to see if your current insurance plan will cover any of the vaccinations. While our insurance plan would not cover any travel related immunizations, they were willing to cover all the routine shots for the kids which saved us over $1000.

Have all immunizations received documented on a travelers' card which should be carried with your passport. If you get a yellow fever vaccination, make sure they write not only the date you received it, but also the manufacturer and batch number of the serum - not having this information can cause a problem. Also be prepared for the fact that no one may ever ask you for this information!

Malaria

A big risk factor with no vaccination is malaria. Some people feel strongly enough about this disease, they refuse to travel to any malaria risk countries. The problem is, you will be ruling out a lot of wonderful travel destinations. The number one way to avoid malaria is to avoid mosquito bites. We carried, from home, mosquito repellent with DEET and sprayed ourselves when necessary. While I don't use DEET spray at home due to its toxicity, the reality is, we don't have malaria at home - under these circumstances its use seemed warranted. Keeping yourself covered by wearing light weight long sleeve shirts and long pants is also a deterrent to mosquito bites.

We also used permethrin, an insect repellent for clothes. In Rome, our last stop before leaving for Africa, we used our two cans of permethrin, brought from home, to spray: two shirts, one pair of pants and two pair of socks for Marty and me and two shirts, two pair of pants and two pair of socks for each of the girls. We carried these sprayed clothes in a plastic bag separate from our other belongings. At dusk, when the mosquitoes come out, we would change into our "sprayed clothes" until bedtime. Often we would wear sprayed clothes without ever spraying ourselves. The spray is effective for up to six washings and since we only used those clothes for the evening, we were able to use them throughout our 3 ½ months of malaria exposure. Once we were no longer in malaria risk countries, we added these clothes back into our regular wardrobe rotation. While your travel doctor may sell permethrin, I found cans to be half the cost at an outdoor store.

Sleeping in mosquito netting is also a deterrent to malaria. As we booked our accommodations in high risk countries we would ask about mosquito netting. If the room had air conditioning, netting was not an issue as we just kept our windows closed. If there was no air conditioning we made sure the accommodation had netting. While there is a small hassle factor dealing with the netting, there is also something exotic about it and Avocet and Siena never tired of sleeping in it as it made them feel like princesses!

While we took these precautions to reduce our risk of being bitten, we were not willing to leave our risk of getting malaria solely to that. We carried a four month supply of malaria pills which we started taking in Rome. Malaria pills come in a variety of "flavors" so begin your research early to determine which pill is best for you and your travel companions. Look into all the possible side effects then talk it over with your doctor and/or travel doctor. Be sure to obtain enough pills prior to leaving to last you through all your malaria risk countries. While you may be able to obtain pills "on the road," it is strongly advised not to do this as you don't know the quality of the pill you are purchasing.

If traveling with children who don't yet swallow pills, there is no time like the present to learn. Nine months prior to leaving (a year prior to hitting our first malaria zone), we began to work with the kids on learning how to swallow pills. We purchased a container of mini M&M's. Three containers and nine months later, we were leaving on a jet plane and neither Siena nor Avocet could consistently swallow the "pills." Up to this point I was laid back about the whole thing, but now, concern is creeping in. In addition to the malaria pills, I was carrying all our OTC medications in pill form, no liquid. If anyone had a headache or fever, they would have to swallow a pill.

We tried cutting "pills" in half, drinking from a straw, swallowing it with yogurt or applesauce; none of these provided consistent results. By the time we hit Venice, we were out of mini M&M's. We would be in Africa in only one month's time! While eating in a restaurant in the Tuscan hill town of San Gimignano, we noticed some ice cream topping that looked like mini M&M's. Whatever they were, they were the right size. We hand motioned to the waiter that we would like to buy a small cup of those "candies." He clearly found it a strange request, but brought over a small cup of the candies anyway at no charge. We were back in business with only ten days to go. In Montepulciano, one week before needing to take their daily pill, Avocet and Siena successfully swallowed "pill" after "pill." My stress level dropped tremendously that day. FYI, worse case scenario, malaria pills can be crushed and put into food, but don't have a very good taste.

When visiting a malaria zone, not all months are equal in risk. While the CDC may recommend you take all precautions against contracting malaria all the time, rainy months inherently have a greater risk. Temperatures will also be a determining factor of risk. We were advised that even in December, southern China was a risk. When we arrived to Yangshou, the temperatures were unusually cold and after one week, we decided our risk of contracting frostbite was greater than our risk of contracting malaria. We stopped taking our malaria pills two weeks earlier than planned.

First Aid Kit for the Road

Remember you are traveling around the globe, not to the moon. There will be stores or farmacias wherever you go. These stores, however, may not be selling what you want, when you need it. And the people in these stores may be speaking a foreign language making getting what you want challenging. While sign language can get you pretty far, it is best to be equipped with a well stocked first aid kit, carrying items you are most likely to need. At the end of your travels, if you come home with your first aid kit still well stocked, consider it a success.

Customize your first aid kit to suit your particular health conditions. Our "generic" first aid kit contained the following:

Tweezers and safety pins
Band aids
Ibuprofen or acetaminophen
Neosporin antibacterial ointment
Non mercury thermometer
Over the counter sleeping aids
Medication for constipation
Medication for diarrhea
Antifungal cream
Antihistamine
Decongestant
Dramamine or other motion sickness medication
Antibiotics for travelers' diarrhea (filled prescriptions – five episodes per person)
Hydrocortisone cream
Anti yeast cream for vaginal infections

Carry these medicines in a Ziploc plastic bag (for waterproofing) and then in another bag for extra protection. To save room, remove some or all of the packaging, making sure each item is easily identifiable and that you have proper dosing instructions. With the exception of the antibiotic prescription, I carried everything in my checked luggage. The prescription, along with our malaria pills, I carried in my backpack which was not checked. Airlines "are not responsible for prescription drugs," so carry all prescriptions in your carry on luggage.

I am pleased that most of these medications came home unused. However, we were glad to have them when we were in need.

Prescriptions

If you are currently taking any prescription medications that you will be continuing to use, obtain enough for the entire length of the trip. Since many pharmacies dispense medications in one month quantities, you will have to ascertain from your doctor and/or pharmacy how to go about this. In addition to carrying the medication, have a copy of the prescription itself in case it's needed.

If you wear eyeglasses, carry an extra pair in your carry on bag as well as a copy of the prescription. The written prescription will come in handy not only if you lose your glasses, but also if you decide to have a pair of glasses made while on the road as many countries offer prescription glasses at a much cheaper cost than what we pay here in the US.

Staying Healthy on the Road

If your time away will be greater than six months, assume you will get sick. If you were home, chances are you would be sick within that time period, so why not expect it while traveling. Still, there are things you can do to help reduce the chances of being ill while on the road.

First and foremost, make sure you are leaving the country in a healthy state. Prior to leaving, everyone traveling should obtain a physical exam, a dental exam and an eye exam. Should any issues come up during these exams, you can take care of them before leaving, change your travel plans (if serious enough), or at least be aware of them and take the necessary precautions. Siena had never worn glasses. During an eye exam two months before leaving, we discovered she was near sighted. We got her glasses and she was able to see the world from a totally different perspective than she would have otherwise.

What is true at home is true on the road; the number one way to help avoid sickness is to wash your hands. This can't be truer than when traveling, especially to countries where sanitation standards are less than what we are used to. We couldn't stress to the kids enough the importance of keeping their hands clean. When soap and water weren't available, we used the hand sanitizer each of us carried in our backpacks. In between washings or sanitization, we stressed the need to keep hands away from the face, especially eyes, ears, nose and mouth.

Wearing a mask while flying is a way to avoid airborne illnesses. This is clearly becoming a more common practice and with the outbreak of swine flu while we were traveling, we saw a lot of this. People who are particularly susceptible to respiratory illnesses find this a great way to reduce risk. Another precaution you can practice while flying is to drink lots of fluids. The air inside an airplane is extremely dry and there is a risk of dehydration. The large quantities of fluids you should be drinking do not include alcoholic or caffeinated beverages which don't hydrate. Bottled water is best. Also while flying, get up and move around or, at a minimum, move your legs around. This will help prevent DVTs, (deep vein thrombosis) - blood clots in the legs. The longer your flight, the greater the risk of DVTs in sedentary legs so get up and talk to your neighbors – at the other end of the plane!

Trust your instincts when it comes to where and what you eat. Each night in Zanzibar, as we headed out to a restaurant for dinner, we would walk down the night market street. There we would see grills set up with all kinds of wonderful things to eat. While we longed to partake of this food, we never did; it just didn't seem like a good idea. On the other hand, we ate lots of street food in Thailand and Laos and never got sick. Lucky? Maybe. But somehow if you trust your gut, (pun intended) you will get a sense of when it's a good idea to eat somewhere and when it's not. This applies not only to street food, but to restaurants as well. When eating on a budget, there are places that are "cleaner" than others and a safer bet.

Travelers' diarrhea is almost inevitable. The foods you are eating are changing regularly and your system is just not used to them. Even with drinking bottled water, which you will do in all but first world countries, your system is going to get upset. This is not a serious form of diarrhea and you should try to avoid treating it medically. Take in ample amounts of water to prevent dehydration and only resort to anti-diarrhea medication if you must travel or an antibiotic if things get more serious. Food choices will obviously affect your risk of travelers' diarrhea and it is typically advised not to eat any unpeeled fruits or vegetables unless they are cooked.

Wearing water shoes is another way to stay healthy. If you aren't familiar with water shoes, they are light weight shoes designed to wear in the water. Not Tevas, Keens or any other type of waterproof sandal, I'm talking about an inexpensive (under $15) nylon upper/rubber bottom shoe. These shoes will protect your feet and keep you from getting cuts and sores as you explore the pebble or stone beaches of the world. In addition, there are several diseases, as well as fungi, you can get through your feet and water shoes can protect you from these potential health problems as well.

What if I Get Sick?

If you do get sick, remember you are traveling Earth, not Mars; doctors are available in all countries. When researching each city you will be staying in, write down the hospital or health clinic listed in the guide book where you might find an English speaking doctor. If you never use that information you have some scrap paper to use once you leave that country. But if you need a doctor, you will find that information invaluable. If you are staying in a hotel or guest house, they might have a doctor on call, or at least be able to refer you to one they have previously used.

Join IAMAT, International Association for Medical Assistance to Travelers, by making a donation at lamat.org. This organization offers free travel health advice including a referral list of doctors and clinics abroad. They will send you a booklet which is a good reference should you need medical assistance while traveling. Be sure to join far enough in advance so they have time to mail you the information needed.

Pharmacies can be incredibly helpful. In the US, we rely on our pharmacists for filling prescriptions, but they are trained to do a lot more than put pills into little bottles. And while many drugs require a prescription in the US, abroad they may not. You can walk into a pharmacy, describe your problem to the pharmacist, and walk out with a drug without ever having seen a doctor.

In Sickness and in Health

If you end up needing a doctor, consider it a cultural experience, because it will be. In a year's time, I sought out a doctor three times. Once in Slovenia because I had sea sickness that was not going away, once in Thailand because I felt an antibiotic I had taken (which I had brought with me) wasn't making me feel better, and once in China because I wanted to experience acupuncture in its native land. All three were positive experiences both medically and culturally. Besides, it gives you something to blog about!

Doctors for Great Prices...

Sunday, August 17, 2008
<u>**DOCTOR, SLOVENIAN STYLE**</u>
Posted by lisa at 6:00 AM

I get motion sick! So riding an overnight ferry from Korcula to Rijeka (in Croatia) for eighteen hours was not my favored form of transportation. I took several Dramamine along the way which makes it OK to travel but I can still feel the movement of the ship. But after a week I was still feeling the movement of the ship and started to wonder if something else was wrong.

I need to add in another fact that makes this all that much more complicated. The night we arrived in Ljubljana, Slovenia, I fell. We were out to dinner and my chair (just my chair, no one else's) was up on an eight inch platform. When I got off the chair and took a step backward to leave, I fell off the platform (not a pretty site). I hit my butt and arm and felt several muscles in other parts of my body strain but I did not hit my head. So when one week later the boat is still rocking in my head, I'm wondering if somehow the fall impacted me more than I think.

My pre-trip research had the name of a health clinic and the Bureau of Tourism confirmed that this would be a good place to go. So Thursday morning I head out to the doctor. I arrive at the clinic and information tells me to go up one floor. Up one floor are lots of doors, lots of chairs, and lots of people waiting but no additional "information person." I head back down and ask again. I am then handed a piece of paper with three room numbers on it and I'm told to knock on one of the three doors, my choice. I then have to choose whether I

want the doctor behind door #1, door #2 or door #3 –
suddenly I'm on "Let's Make a Deal." I opt for room 143
because it's the first room number I come to. A woman opens
the door and speaks to me in Slovene. I ask if she knows
English and she says, "a little". I tell her I would like to see a
doctor. She asks for my passport, takes it, indicates I should
wait in the waiting room and then closes the door. Now I'm on
"Let's Make a Deal" and they're holding my passport hostage!
I wait for forty five min. to one hour and they call me in. The
doctor spoke some English and was very nice. She did a basic
neurological exam and seemed to feel that everything was OK
and was convinced that I was still feeling the consequences
from the ship rocking which could easily last that long she
says. She gave me a prescription which I could take to help
stabilize my head until things improve on their own. For this
examination I paid full price since I am not a Slovene Citizen,
7.75E (approximately $11.50 US). I then filled my
prescription, again for full price, to the tune of 15.00E
(about $22.50 US). Both of these costs are less than what I
would have paid at home for my co-pay as a fully insured
individual! MAKES YOU WONDER!!!!

We never thought that four people traveling for a year could
make it through an entire year without needing a doctor, at
least once. I wasn't expecting it to be so soon or for
something as mundane as a motion sickness hangover. I'm
hoping for a speedy recovery and for all future health issues
to go as well as this one did!

Five Star Health Care...

Tuesday, December 23, 2008
SCHEDULE YOUR NEXT MEDICAL PROCEDURE HERE

Posted by lisa at 5:45 AM

Toward the end of our stay in Nong Khai, Thailand, I wasn't feeling well. I took some medicine that I carry with me but I didn't seem to be feeling better. Upon arriving in Bangkok, I decided to go to the doctor – mostly because I figured this would be a better move than waiting until we went to China, only five days later. According to my research, as well as the recommendation of our hotel, I went to the Bumrungrad Hospital where I was told I would find an English speaking doctor.

I found more than an English speaking doctor. I found an international hospital that was like a five star hotel! A person immediately greeted me in English and inquired as to my needs. I was sent to the 10th floor where I was again greeted by an English speaking person who directed me to registration. I was rapidly registered, using state of the art computer equipment, and told which floor to proceed to. Passing by the Starbucks (I was tempted to stop but didn't), I went to the 16th floor and waited to see the doctor. In the waiting area you could hear languages from all over the world as people come here from everywhere to receive first class medical treatment – sometimes at a fraction of the cost of what it would cost in their own country. I had heard about medical tourism on NPR, but now I was seeing it first hand.

The good humored doctor I saw spoke English very well. My lab test came out negative and he felt that I needed to give the antibiotic treatment a little more time. Hearing that I was leaving soon and heading to China, he prescribed an alternative antibiotic for me to carry in case I didn't feel better within a week. For his time, I was charged 500 Baht ($14.08 US), a facility fee of 200 Baht ($5.63 US) and a lab fee of 200 Baht (also $5.63 US). This was less than my health insurance co-pay at home and all at a first class medical facility.

Before leaving the hospital, I stopped in Au Bon Pain on the first floor to pick up some desperately needed "American Style" chocolate chip cookies for the family. As I looked around, it was clear to me that this would be the ideal place to have a future medical procedure performed. And recuperating in Thailand after the procedure wouldn't be too bad either!

Chapter Fourteen

WHAT IN THE WORLD DO I PACK?

Prior to our leaving, we were often asked, "How do you pack for a whole year?" The answer is, "The same way you pack for a week, only a little less, and a lot more carefully."

We each had a 28" rolling duffel bag and a day pack. The duffel bag could be converted into a backpack if necessary. If your backs are strong and your kids are big enough, backpacks have a definite advantage. They are easier to manage: getting in and out of buses, trains, and ferries, roaming streets, etc. With backs that are not youthful and kids that are small, we didn't consider backpacks. Having a rolling bag was perfect as everyone could "pull their own weight." You want to travel with as small a bag as possible; even a 28" duffel bag got to be a hassle dragging it everywhere for a full year, especially up steps.

Don't cheap out on your bag. It's going to get a work out – by you, the airlines, the cobblestone streets, the porters in Africa and India that you didn't even ask for. It holds all your worldly possessions and you want it to last. If you have had luck with a brand you previously used, stick with it. If not, look at reviews and find a new product. If your bag falls apart, chances are, it will be at the most inconvenient time, in a country that offers the fewest options for replacement.

Before putting anything into your bag, ask yourself these questions:

> ➤ Do I really need this or do I just want it?
> ➤ Does this item have multiple purposes?
> ➤ Does this item have staying power, i.e. will I still like it/need it six months from now?

What in the World Do I Pack?

Consider climate. Planning your trip with weather in mind will reduce your need for different clothes. We left the US in June and returned in June and did our best to seek mild temperatures, visiting countries in their spring, summer and fall seasons. This worked out very well. We did have some colder days, but were able to handle those by layering clothes versus packing for a colder climate. We met another family who wanted to take advantage of winter activities. They designed their itinerary to visit colder climates first, mailed home their winter clothes and then proceeded with only their lighter weight articles.

Another option is second hand stores. They are not everywhere and you can't always find what you want, but they remain a viable option. We shopped second hand stores to trade off old clothes for "new." They can be used to handle a weather wardrobe shortfall. You can pack for warmer climates and then add heavier clothes as needed. You can recycle clothes back to the second hand store or donate to an appreciative local when you move on to different weather conditions.

Don't think of climate in isolation of culture. It may be hot in Tanzania, but locals do not wear shorts. If you're white, you will stick out in Tanzania. But you don't want to exacerbate that by wearing culturally inappropriate clothes. Bring clothes suitable to both the climate and the culture.

Shoes are a biggy. They are heavy and take up a lot of room, but are one of the most important items in your bag. They will be worn constantly and you will be doing more walking than you ever have before. I searched for months before I found the shoes I wanted to bring. Shoes need to be comfortable, supportive, fashionable, versatile and inexpensive (not!). Cheap out some place else but not on your feet. Remember to get your shoes enough in advance so you can break them in before leaving home. You don't want to be trying to soften those leather uppers on the cobblestones of Europe.

Kids' shoes work the other way. Get them as close to leaving as possible, allowing the minimum time to break them in. Hopefully they won't need new shoes three weeks into the trip.

It's not only kids' feet that are growing, it's their bodies as well. Shirts that are a little "looser" with some growing room will serve them well. And if you haven't discovered children's adjustable pants, now is the time. These pants have an elastic adjustment on the inside so you can make the waistline tighter or looser. As the kids grow, you can let the elastic out. Pants that roll up into capris are a great idea. They can wear them as long pants or capris. As they grow, and the pants get shorter, rolling the pants up helps prevent them from looking like pants that are too short.

Here is what I packed for a year.

Long Pants – 3 pair
Shorts – 3 pair
Long Sleeve Shirts – 4
Short Sleeve Shirts – 4
Sleeveless Shirts – 4
Underpants – 7
Bras – 3
Socks – 7
Casual Dresses (below the knee) – 2
Long Skirt – 1
Bathing Suit – 1
Sandals – 1 pair
Walking Shoes – 1 pair
Water Shoes – 1 pair
Rain Jacket – 1
Fleece Jacket – 1
Silk Long Underwear (top and bottom) – 1 pair
P.J.'s or nightshirt – 1 pair
Toiletry Bag
    Comb & brush
    Toothbrush with cover, toothpaste and floss
    Shampoo
    Soap dish with soap
    Razor with extra blades
    Nail clippers and nail file
    Ear plugs
    Q-tips
    Make-up
    Hair accessories
    Hair mousse
    Deodorant
    Pocket Knife

What in the World Do I Pack?

Tampons and/or sanitary napkins
5 pair silver earrings
Hat
First aid kit
Sewing kit
Writing journal with extra pens and pencils
Books
Sun screen
Bug spray and Permethrin
Glasses (along with an extra pair and the prescription)
Sun glasses
Prescription medicines
Water bottle
Binoculars
Playing cards and dice game
3 Cameras, batteries and transfer cord
Art supplies
Spray and Wash Stick
Ziploc Bags
MP3 players and charger
MP3 speaker box (converts MP3 player to a stereo)
Laptop computer and accessories
Worldwide plug adaptor kit (for electrical items)
Binders with all trip research
All important papers: passports, tickets, health cards etc.
Money belt and cash
Checkbook

This list obviously varied slightly from person to person in our family. Marty felt no need to bring dresses or bras but wanted more socks. The kids' clothes, on the other hand, were so small, that they got to bring more of everything.

More Stuff About The Stuff You Bring

Anytime you find something that is multipurpose, you save room for something else. Marty had only zip-off pants which served as shorts. Two out of three of my pants could be rolled into capris. One of my long sleeve cotton shirts could serve as a bathing suit cover up. Water shoes doubled as shower shoes when you came across a bathroom that looked a little less clean.

Buy yourself hanging toiletry bags. This way, everyone can keep their toiletry bag in the bathroom when no counter room is available.

Don't bother with travel size toiletries. For any length of time, a travel size shampoo is not going to cut it. Get used to the idea of carrying full size personal care products. Each person need not carry their own as one of each product is sufficient for the family. Carry these larger size toiletry items in your checked luggage, not your carry on. Your checked luggage is also where you should carry your pocket knife. I stored my Swiss army knife in my toiletry bag on travel days. When I reached a destination and unpacked, I took my knife out of the toiletry bag and placed it in the day pack. It was indispensible. The trick, however, is to remember to reverse your steps so that on flight days, the knife is no longer in your day pack. This system worked flawlessly for nine months, until we reached the airport in Rapi Nui (see Once Was Lost but Now It's Found, October 20, 2009 at Oneworldonetrip.blogspot.com)

Women who are still menstruating have a decision to make. Carry enough tampons and/or sanitary napkins for the entire trip or go with whatever you can find along the way. Women all over the world menstruate, so it's not like you won't find anything; it just may not be what you had in mind. In larger cities you will find familiar looking products but often of lesser quality and more expense. I opted for a middle of the road approach. I brought enough tampons to last me until Australia. There I was sure to find something to my liking. At that point I replenished for the remainder of the trip. You may also want to bring condoms, contraceptives and sexual lubricants.

We brought two money belts, around the neck for me and around the waist for Marty. The key to money belts is to use them; they don't work effectively if they are sitting in your suitcase while you are out and about. We were good about using them on travel days, but became complacent with their use day to day. We eventually paid the price for this "relaxed" attitude and quickly got back in the habit of using them.

If you can do without something, do. At home, I blow dry my hair and use three different hair care products. On the road, I went sans blow dryer and had only one hair care product. My hair did not look perfect everyday – but then, neither did I. I did without my facial wash, moisturizer, body lotion and make-up. I took one blusher and a tube of mascara for those occasions I felt the desire to "dress up."

Consider leaving your jewelry at home. Anything that is valuable should be in a safe deposit box at your bank and not in your travel bag or on your body. Marty and I wore wedding bands only. I had no necklaces or bracelets - only a few pair of silver earrings. Jewelry is a good souvenir since it takes up no room, so it won't be long before you have some foreign bling.

Typically your everyday items will do, but sometimes a specialty item is needed. Women's panties are petite but men's boxers are room hoggers. Marty bought silk boxers which took up one third the space. They needed to be hand washed and by the end, they were rags, but they were well worth it.

Winner of the most valued item award was an unlikely candidate, our Spray and Wash Stick. With a limited number of clothes, a permanent food stain on a pair of pants can reduce your pants allowance by 33%. Laundry facilities may not be readily available. Using our Spray and Wash Stick, we were able to "save" our clothes from looking like a "Who ate what where road map." We quickly realized how precious this item was and that one stick was not going to carry us for a full year. We asked my Mother to bring one when she visited us in Poland. She brought an instant stain remover pen which is not the same. Marty's brother was to mail us a package in Australia and once again we asked for a Spray and Wash Stick (ours was now down to the dregs). Once again we got instant spot treatment sticks. Nice tries by our family members but failures on both attempts. Next time, we will take two sticks.

The most valued item runner up was Ziploc Bags. Originally, these were used for anything that could get messy: sun screen, shampoo, soap, etc. I stashed extras in my duffle pocket at the time of packing. These were constantly used to protect our travel bags from spills, but also to keep food fresh, pack picnic lunches, store snacks and carry food items from one country to the next. They were washed and reused hundreds of times. We looked in supermarkets for replacements but never found them until we were in Chile, 10½ months into our trip. If it's a specialty item, don't count on finding it in other countries.

What We Wished We Had Brought

Everything we brought was well used and there was nothing we could have done without. I would have exchanged a pair of shorts for an additional dress (for cultural reasons) but that's about it. There were, however, a few items we hadn't brought that we wished we had. The first is a good small flashlight. We subsequently bought one in Thailand, but it was cheap and didn't last long. The second was a pair of quality ear plugs. Around the world many things wake you up (or keep you up): roosters, church bells, Moslem calls to prayer, delivery trucks, music, traffic, dogs howling... We thought we were prepared by bringing along the "carrots" as my kids called them — a large bag of orange disposable foam ear plugs. They were worthless! We attempted a new purchase in New Zealand, but those didn't work out either. Invest in a good pair.

Will You Get Sick of Your Clothes?

Marty did! He even wrote a blog about it. The girls and I, however, never got sick of our clothes. Strangely, instead of feeling tired of the same outfits, I enjoyed the simplicity. If it was cool out, I wore one of three pairs of pants. If it was hot, one of three pairs of shorts. No walking into a closet full of clothes saying "What am I going to wear today?" Shoes? "Do I need open toed or closed toed?" was the only question I needed to ask myself. As for matching, my shoes matched everything (both in my mind and in reality). Now that I am home and have the expanded version of my wardrobe, I still find myself wearing the same things over and over. I liked the simplicity of my travel wardrobe and have carried over the habit of "re-wearing" my clothes.

Stuff About the Stuff You Pick Up Along the Way

Some items will be for temporary use while others will become permanent fixtures in your bag. Some will be replacements for things you are now out of: shampoo, soap, pens, etc; other items will be totally new.

To mail our first package from Montepulciano, Italy, we needed a roll of packing tape. Packing tape does not come in small containers, so the roll of packing tape traveled with us, used every time we mailed a package.

In Europe, our apartments had a washing machine and drying rack. From Africa through China, however, we had only laundry services. Some things we just wanted to hand wash, but where to dry them? Avocet wanted string for one of her projects, so when we came across a ball of twine, we bought it for her. Before you know it, we were borrowing twine from her to make clotheslines to hang our hand wash. Eventually she handed us the ball of twine, acknowledging that we needed it a lot more.

While in apartments, we bought food to cook. Unless you enjoy eating bland food, you need spices. Even a limited supply of spices can get pricy if you have to replace them every time you switch locations. We bought spices in small packages, later carrying them in Ziploc bags in our checked luggage. For the first three months of our trip, I carried around: salt, pepper, oregano, basil, thyme and cinnamon. It took up little space, added no weight and was a good cost saver and big convenience. Other items that transferred locations were: coffee, tea bags, laundry soap (preferably powder form), dish soap and paper products. Extra snack items were carried in our backpacks to eat while traveling.

I drink only decaf coffee which was not easy and sometimes impossible to find. When we found it, we bought extra to carry with us. But ground coffee doesn't always guarantee you a cup of coffee; you need some way to make it. Some apartments had a coffee maker, drip pot, espresso pot or French press, but not all. In a small hardware shop in Pienza, Italy, Marty found a drip cone and filters, he was thrilled! With a cone and filter you need only boiling water for a fresh cup of coffee. We bought the cone and filters and carried them for the remaining nine months of our trip, saying good bye to our faithful companions at our last stop in Quito, Ecuador. The cone was bulky (but not heavy) to carry, but once we stuffed it with some socks or underwear, it didn't take up much room. When we switched to guest houses and hotels, we were still able to enjoy a cup of coffee since we often had a hot pot to boil water in. No replacement filters? Just use a paper towel.

While in apartments, we never had to buy cleaning supplies other than laundry and dish soap and sponges, but we did need toilet paper. Some apartments came with a lifetime supply but most came with one or two rolls. Even if you are not staying in apartments, you will need toilet paper, at least one roll. Crush the roll, put it in a clean plastic bag and carry it in your day pack at all times. You'll definitely need it in some places!

One Last Item

Our selection of short sleeved shirts included a "trip shirt." (See T-Shirts for Short Memories, January 26, 2008 at Oneworldonetrip.blogspot.com). Many companies produce inexpensive custom t-shirts and will design a logo at no additional cost. The front had our logo and trip name "One World One Trip" and the back had our itinerary, the 2008-2009 Tour. At the end of our stay in each location we visited, we took a picture, in a favorite spot, wearing our trip shirts. We now have great pictures and our souvenir t-shirts!

Don't Let This Happen to You...

Wednesday, January 14, 2009
I HATE MY CLOTHES
Posted by Marty at 4:30 AM

Can you imagine wearing the same clothes over and over? It gets really old. In fact I "HATE" most of the stuff that I have to put on each and every day. What seemed novel in May 2008 in prep for the trip is not so novel now. We all planned ahead and bought clothes that were multi purpose, such as zip off pants (which convert to shorts) that are made out of synthetic materials which wash and dry quickly. And that crappy black stretch belt that matches it, ugghhhh!!! We "layer" also. I wear t-shirts under one of my three long sleeve shirts. I dislike my clothes even more now because earlier, with variable weather, we were mixing shorts and pants. Since we arrived in China, it's only been the long pants and layered shirts. And those zip offs do nothing for my figure? Notice the next person on the street with "travel pants" and you will notice a belly that plops over the belt AND a baggy butt. The two 600 ml beers per day have nothing to do with my belly. It's the damn pants. I have worn the same royal blue L.L. Bean fleece jacket that I was so proud of when purchased back in April, for the last twenty five days without fail. AARRRGGGH!!!!!

This seems such a petty grievance. Get over it Marty. Remember the people that have less.....Nah, I just want to complain.....

I'll go on....I have a pair of New Balance cross-trainers that are very comfortable, until you wear them for weeks on end. A podiatrist friend of mine said you should wear different shoes each day and not the same pair day in and day out. I see all these people with neat shoes....Chucks, cool Nike casual shoes and I'm stuck with my old pair that incidentally (planned) match all three of my boring pair of pants.

When in Sydney I want to go shopping for new clothes that will make me feel hip, new and invigorated and sexy. I want clothes that take off the extra ten kilos I have been packing for years. No more travel clothes. Stylish pants with a belt that takes up too much room in the suitcase will be the order of the day. Orange colors, silver emblems, even shirts that say "Billabong" will be on my shelves. And I will shod myself in a brand spanking new pair of black leather Chucks (Converse All-Stars) regardless of what my podiatrist might think. I just won't tell him. So what if my arches need surgery...I'm having a fashion crisis!!!! Help. Besides, I need new clothes to match the shaved head. Soon you will meet Marty, the stylin' man.

Stayed tuned in a month for me bitching about my new wardrobe.

Chapter Fifteen

COMMUNICATION AND TECHNOLOGY –
LINKS TO THE OTHER SIDE OF THE WORLD

I remember when communication while traveling meant sending a post card, reminding those at home you were some place wonderful and they were not. Communication on the road was pretty much one way. If someone needed to send you something, it was sent "poste restante", (the post office holding the letter or package until your arrival). Occasionally you made an expensive long distance phone call. Those days are LONG GONE.

One of our biggest debates was whether or not to take a laptop computer. We were both undecided; Marty leaning towards having one while I was inclined the other way. My list of concerns: it was one more thing to keep up with, it will get ripped of, people will spend too much time on it. I also feared we would become so dependent on it that if we couldn't use it (no Internet service, no electricity, it was lost or stolen) we would be lost. OK, I am going to put it in print, I WAS WRONG! Taking a computer was the best thing we did. It beat even the Spray and Wash Stick. <u>Everything</u> would have been more challenging without it.

We bought a Dell 11.3" laptop with an external CD drive and used it for checking and sending emails, keeping a blog, loading pictures, uploading pictures online, travel research, educational research, schooling, watching movies, phone calls. We bought a used laptop so if it was lost or stolen, we wouldn't lose a brand new expensive machine. Computers are cheaper (and smaller) than ever so your options will be many. All portables should run on any electrical current used around the world, but ask before buying.

If you don't carry a computer, you will have to rent a computer (going to Internet cafes.) When you think about this option, consider how many Internet cafes you have in your neighborhood. None? How many do you have in your city? Not too many? None at all? The more affluent a country's population, the more people own computers, the less need for Internet cafes. There are exceptions to this. Some well touristed areas have Internet sites despite the countries' favorable economic circumstances. Others will have few. Besides availability, there are other issues to consider: How much per hour will you spend? What are the hours of operation? How long will you wait for a computer? How convenient is the location? What type of speed will you have and how long will it take you to do something?

All these issues don't disappear when you have a computer. You still need a signal to use the Internet. And chances are, your speed isn't greater than what's available at the local Internet site. You can, however, maximize your use of that slow speed. Uploading pictures to a website was the most time consuming task we had. When we were dependent on an Internet café, it was also one of the most frustrating. If we had an Internet signal available at our accommodation, we would set our pictures to upload and go to bed. In the morning, our pictures were where we wanted them. Very few Internet cafes allow you to sleep in them while you upload your pictures.

Our computer gave us freedom but also hassles. The hard drive crashed in Poland and had to be replaced. Later it needed work in New Zealand. Each event required us to find someone who could fix it. Marty and I were not the most computer literate and it would have been helpful to know more about the equipment we were carrying. Learn as much as you can about your computer so you are not at the mercy of others when problems occur. Be prepared for a crash. Carry your operating system disk and any other programs you must have. If there is a problem, you will be able to restore your computer to its previous state.

Think about how you will want to use your computer and make sure you have all the peripherals needed for those tasks. Planning on using Skype? You will need a head set and maybe a camera. Uploading pictures? You'll want a transfer cable for your camera. Other items that are useful or necessary: an extra battery, electric cord with worldwide adaptors, MP3 player charger attachment and flash drives.

Skype

The word Skype is my generic term for using your computer as a telephone to make calls – FOR FREE. Familiarize yourself with Skype or another computer phone system and choose one. I was skeptical, but after strong recommendations from someone who had spent three months in Europe with her family, I decided to download it to our laptop. It's free, simple to download and easy to use. You can make free calls to anyone around the world who has the same messaging system. Therefore, plan ahead - these things are easier to do before leaving town. Contact those you might want to call and ask them to download the same messaging system you have. Before we left, I had my mother and sister add Skype and we had two friends who already had it. By the end of the trip, I had asked an additional five or six people to download it.

Although Skype is available at most Internet cafes around the world, you have to deal with the operating hours of the Internet site. While this doesn't seem like a problem now, it becomes one as you move time zones and find yourself hours away from home. It's 10:00 AM and the Internet cafe is open, but do you want to be calling your mother at 3:00 AM her time?

Skype gives you the opportunity to talk with non-Skype users on a fee basis. This includes land lines as well as mobile phones. You open an account, deposit money into this account and draw on this account as you make your calls. The rates are extremely competitive. We thought we would have no use for this and didn't deposit any money into an account. Then, my mother got sick and was no longer at home near her computer with Skype. Instead she was in a hospital and then a nursing home with only a phone line. I tried adding money to our Skype account while overseas, but it didn't work. I recommend establishing an account and adding dollars to it while still in the US even if you don't think you will use it! You never know what will happen and it's better to have $15.00 sitting in an account waiting to be used, than the inability to reach someone when you need to.

Skype phone calls were a great way to stay in touch when we needed to and a nice way to connect with friends and family when we were feeling disconnected or wanted an update on what was happening at home. When Avocet and Siena started really missing their friends, I set up Skype "play dates" via their friend's parents so they could have a half hour conversation with one of their buddies. On their 10th birthday in Chiang Mai, Thailand, we set up a virtual birthday party with their friends, arranging a series of phone calls, one after the other. They loved it and it was a great way to start off their first birthday away from home. We found it best to email people first to set up a time and date for a call rather than use the hit or miss method. In the email, establish the time (being specific about time zones), who will initiate the call and, in the case of a dropped call, who's responsibility it is to call back. If you don't do this, you both could be trying to call each other and get busy signals.

If you think you don't want to keep in touch at this level, my suggestion is to set up an account with a computer phone system anyway. If you never use it, fine. For me it turned out to be a life saver. Three months into our trip, my mother needed to have brain surgery. For the next nine months, Skype was my link to my mother's health. While my sister told me not to come home, she also knew I was just a phone call away – a great comfort to both of us.

Emails

We each had our own email account. When you are on the road together for a long time, there isn't much privacy. Email accounts can be private. Individual accounts also prevent "accidents" from happening: others deleting needed information, misplaced communications, etc. The fewer opportunities for these "screw ups," the better.

Technology Safety

Our computer was our lifeline. On travel days, we packed it, and all peripherals, in a safely guarded backpack. This is important. If you pack your power cord in your suitcase, and your suitcase is lost or stolen, then you're on battery power until you can replace the cord (which could be a long time). In apartments, we left the computer unlocked as no one else had access to the place. When in a guest house, hotel or hostel, we locked the computer to a piece of furniture with a computer lock. Was the locking necessary? No idea. Most of the time, we felt our personal belongings were safe. But we figured that it was better to err on the side of caution than to be sorry.

With respect to technology, your hardware isn't the only thing you want to protect. Protecting your data is equally important. Any documents that are crucial should be backed up on a flash drive carried separate from your computer. Don't store user I.D.'s or passwords in the computer. While this feature saves you from the impossible task of remembering each and every user I.D. and password, it also makes it easy for someone else to access your personal data. We carried a little notebook with all that information in a safely guarded backpack, separate from the computer.

Cameras

Pictures involve more than simply packing a camera. We spent an inordinate amount of time investigating this issue and I wish we had taken more.

What camera are you going to take? Rather than risk our older camera failing us, we purchased two new cameras. Attempting to keep things easy, we purchased the newer/upgraded version of our existing camera, figuring we already knew how to use that brand. While that turned out to be true, new research would have led to better choices. We weren't happy with our cameras. About five months into the trip, we decided we needed a camera with a much better zoom, desiring to take pictures of people without being invasive. Marty did the research, but at that point we were in Thailand and the cameras were expensive there. The choice was to cough up the extra bucks or figure out how to get one from the US. Marty's brother obtained the camera and then mailed it to our apartment in Sydney, Australia, several weeks prior to our scheduled arrival. When we reached Sydney, it was waiting for us at the local post office, complete with some American chocolate and his attempt at a Spray and Wash Stick. Fortunately we had a great camera for the second half of our trip! Wish we would have had it for our African safari.

How many cameras do you need? That depends on how many are traveling and who's interested in being a photographer. Are your kids seeking a new hobby? Do you anticipate sightseeing separately some days? We began with three figuring that if we split up, we'd need a second camera, plus our old camera came along as a backup. We typically used just one camera since we found it easier to keep pictures in chronological order that way. Early on, Avocet developed an interest in taking pictures. We gave her one camera and kept the other for our use. If we split up, each group had a camera. After the new camera arrived, the allocation was one to Avocet, the new one for our use and two on the bottom of the suitcase. Keeping our replaced camera later turned out to be fortuitous as we started having problems uploading pictures from our new camera and could use the old one for that purpose. Sometimes it's worth keeping things even when you think you won't need them any longer.

Cameras don't need film but they do need batteries and you go through a lot of battery power on a long trip. We brought sixteen rechargeable batteries stored in plastic battery cases which keep them lasting longer. Purchase high quality batteries and a worldwide battery charger. Since a worldwide charger works off of any electrical current, you won't need a converter - only plug adaptors so that you can plug it in to the various receptacles.

What to do with the multitude of pictures we were going to accumulate was a huge concern. While there were plenty of storage options available, our concern was risk of loss: pictures stored on a camera or computer that was lost, stolen or malfunctioning, pictures burned onto CDs or stored on extra photo cards, mailed home but never received. We did not want to lose our pictures! We figured the best way to safeguard our photos was to upload them to a website where they could be stored away from our physical possessions.

Uploading pictures to an online storage site was time consuming but worth it. While traveling, we heard sad stories of pictures lost - sometimes just a day's worth but other times a lot more. We have all our pictures due to our online storage site and our diligence in executing the rules we set up for ourselves. Each night we uploaded pictures from our camera to our computer. We then uploaded certain photos to KodakGallery.com, our chosen online storage site. Depending on the Internet speed, this upload could go pretty quickly or take half the night. Our policy was to not delete pictures from our camera until the pictures were safely uploaded to Kodak. This way, our photos were stored in two locations, the camera and the computer. Once safely online, we deleted them from the camera but continued to leave them on the computer. Even when our hard drive crashed in Poland, we didn't lose any of our 12,000+ pictures because of these safety measures.

Online storage sites are a great way to share your pictures with those at home. On KodakGallery.com, we made a "Trip Group" of friends, and in one action, we sent a photo album out to 50+ people. Advanced research as to which service to use is worth your time. We had been using KodakGallery.com for years so it seemed a natural choice. In the past, we typically printed pictures for photo albums; we didn't take into consideration that we would be using Kodak differently this time around. After uploading, we would painstakingly edit our pictures and then title each one so we knew what and where it was. This was an arduous task, but we justified it telling ourselves there was no way we would remember everything after a year. We also knew it would be easier to deal with pictures one album at a time than to come home to over 7600 pictures (the number we sent to Kodak). A bonus to titling the photos was that those at home looking at the pictures would know what they were looking at. Now at home, we've discovered that the titles we so painstakingly added do not transfer onto any medium at all. Hours upon hours of work for naught. Had we done more homework, we would have gone with another storage site that could have preserved our titles.

Extensive pre-trip research isn't foolproof. It can only provide you with the best possible solution <u>at the time you are making your decision</u>. This data may not even last the length of your trip. While on the road, Kodak changed their policy regarding the storage of pictures. When we left, storage was free of charge. They then decided to start charging for their storage if you weren't actively making purchases (which of course, we weren't).

We didn't mind paying the fee, but it was all a bit confusing how the plan was being implemented and we spent a lot of time sorting out the details during online chats with Kodak. Kodak also changed their "sharing" format while we were on our trip to a smaller photo frame which we didn't like. Regardless of how much research and preparation you do, there is no guarantee that everything is going to work out the way you want. Flexibility was one of those "life lessons" we were challenged with regularly.

Cell Phones

If you are traveling to one or two countries, using a mobile phone is simple. If you are planning to visit many countries (we visited seventeen), the best option is to pick up a phone and SIM card in each of the countries you visit.

You've had one for years and you can't imagine living without it, right? You may discover otherwise. We never had a cell phone during our year of travel and I found it freeing. There were a few times where it would have been convenient to have one, like when Marty and I got separated - but then we would have needed two! For the most part, we got along perfectly well without one.

This time away is not just about what you are going toward, but also about what you're leaving behind. The technology you bring along should be purposeful, not just out of habit. If you don't really <u>need</u> it, leave it behind, and feel the freedom of having one less thing to answer to.

Nothing Technical About This...

Thursday, January 1, 2009
FLUSHING OUT THE TRUTH ABOUT CHINA
Posted by lisa at 7:15 PM

We encountered our first one in Dubrovnik, Croatia, and walked away. Once we arrived in Africa and later India, we encountered more and they were harder to ignore but often we did. Now that we're in China, it's pretty much impossible to avoid. I'm talking about the infamous squat toilet! Easterners have been using them forever but for us Westerners, it's just hard to get used to them. I don't know why it should be such a big thing, essentially we squat to go to the bathroom anyway; we're just used to doing it with a seat underneath us. Of course, when we visit a less than clean restroom at home, we don't sit, we squat - so it's kind of like the same thing right?

Our hotel has a "Western Style" toilet which means that it looks like a Western toilet, it flushes like a Western toilet but it can't handle paper like a Western toilet. You therefore must wipe and dispose of your paper into a waste bin and not into the toilet. It sounds a little gross, but it's not all that bad. The bin has a lid so it doesn't smell and they empty the bin everyday. Once you leave the hotel however, it's pretty much squat toilets everywhere.

In a decent restaurant, the squat toilet is not too bad since it is clean and doesn't smell bad. They clean the "toilet room" quite frequently, but they use water to clean the whole bathroom and they don't dry the floor afterwards. This causes a small problem, how to pull your pants down to use the squat toilet but not end up with the bottom of your pant legs all wet. Clearly you attempt to do this by holding on to

135

your pants with one hand while you go to the bathroom and then wipe. You can often successfully get this far but then you are stuck with toilet paper in one hand, your pants in the other hand and you have to both pull up your pants and get rid of the toilet paper. The toilet paper bin often has a foot pedal but have you ever tried to push on the pedal of a trash can to open it while your pants are around your thighs and you're trying to hold the bottom of your pants legs up to keep them from getting wet from the floor? The other option is to pull up your pants with one hand while you hold the paper in the other which then frees up your foot to push the pedal to open the can to put your paper in. Clearly we will not be in China long enough to master this art but we are getting better at it.

Public restrooms are another matter. Just like at home where public restrooms can be pretty dicey, the same is true here, only worse! Squat toilets have no water sitting in them so if someone does their "business" in the toilet and doesn't flush, it is there to stink up the entire bathroom. Plus, these bathrooms are not cleaned regularly. I tried a public restroom just once. I walked in, gagged so bad from the stench, that I left and swore that I would rather use the side of the road if necessary.

The good news is that it is cold outside and no one is drinking a whole lot of water. Hot tea would be good but it is caffeinated so we don't drink much of that either. This keeps our "needs" down to a minimum. The bad news is, practice makes perfect and I guess this is one thing that we just won't perfect!

Chapter Sixteen

FINANCES ON THE ROAD AND AT HOME

Life on the road requires a split personality. You have to take care of your day to day finances, as well as those of the life you left behind. Thanks to computers and the Internet, it's easy, requiring only advanced planning and organization. I recommend you have a money market and checking account at the same bank. You can keep the bulk of your funds in the higher interest bearing account and make transfers between the two accounts for easy bill payment. By law, money market accounts are limited in the number of transactions per month. We set ours up so that on the first of the month, a fixed amount automatically transferred from the money market account to the checking account, refreshing it to cover our expenses on the road as well as at home. Cash can always be transferred back to the money market account should there be a balance build up on the checking account side. (No restrictions on deposits into a money market) These accounts should be set up for online accessibility.

Start to mechanize bill payments now. Bills which need to be paid in your absence can be either automatically deducted from your checking account or payable (e-bill) online. Automatic deduction requires less supervision and no computer access. E-bills give you more control and oversight but you need Internet access. Set up monthly bills as well as those that get paid quarterly, semi-annually or annually: auto, life and disability insurance, real estate taxes, etc. All credit cards can be paperless so you receive e-bills and make payments via electronic fund transfers directly from your checking account.

You will find that fewer places around the world take credit cards and if they do, they often charge you the 2% (or more) fee that they get charged. Chances are you won't be using your cards that much. That doesn't mean you shouldn't carry them. They are great for emergencies and for times when you can use them without incurring the additional expense, like making airline ticket purchases. Which credit cards should you carry? Some places take MasterCard, while others take VISA. Most take both and far fewer take American Express. Almost all these cards charge a foreign transaction fee in addition to the current exchange rate. Check your credit card provider's rules to see what they charge. Before leaving home, I found all of our credit card companies charged a foreign transaction fee. Eventually I discovered Capital One did not and applied for a MasterCard, while Marty applied for a VISA. We used these cards for the entire trip in order to avoid the foreign transaction fees. In addition to our new cards, we carried some of our old cards so that both Marty and I had a full set of cards: MasterCard, VISA and American Express. Each card was an independent account so that if any card was lost, the other card would not be compromised in anyway. For this luxury we paid annual fees on four cards, but at the time, we felt the extra security was worth it. Check with your credit card company to see if you can have a spousal card on the same account that can act independently. If they can assure you of this, you could save on annual fees. Were I to leave home without one of the cards listed it would be, you guessed it, the American Express card. Hardly anyone accepted it and we could have saved ourselves $300 in annual membership fees. American Express – yes, you can leave home without it!

On the road we obtained local currency via our ATM Cards. Banks typically charge a fee when you withdraw money using an ATM card and many charge an international service fee on top of that. These fees add up quickly. Shop around within your bank as well as with other banks. We were able to shift our money to a different type of account which incurred no ATM withdrawal fees (international or otherwise). We saved literally hundreds of dollars of fees by having searched for that type of account.

Both Marty and I had an ATM card. If your bank is willing to issue you an extra card for the road, take it; we never thought to ask. Your ATM card is one of the most important things you will carry. It is your primary source for cash on the road. Yes, you have other ways to obtain cash in case of an emergency, but none of those are convenient. You can carry the extra card in a location different from your other cards as a security blanket. For the first ten months of our trip we used Marty's ATM card, considering mine the backup. Then the inevitable happened. Marty was pickpocketed on the Buenos Aires subway. The lucky thief made away with not only Argentinean Pesos, but also Marty's credit cards, driver's license and ATM card. We were able to cancel the credit cards immediately and notified the bank of the lost ATM card. But without an address where they could send a new card, we were unable to replace the missing ATM card. My ATM card became THE card with no backup. Fortunately, we only had two months left when this happened. Still, it was disconcerting not having a backup card.

When using your ATM card to withdraw cash, use only ATM machines attached to banks, no stand alone machines. Cover the key pad with your hand as you punch in your pin code so your code can't be detected by a camera or a watchful eye. Avoid ATMs in areas that are either overly busy or deserted. These are all standard rules. We developed a few new rules of our own based on an incident in Italy almost four months into our trip.

While staying in Montepulciano, we took a day trip to Chiusi, about forty minutes away and needed some Euros. Following the rules above, we found an ATM machine and proceeded to transact our business. Half way through the transaction, the machine shut down, dispensing no cash and eating our ATM card. It was Saturday so the bank was closed. A helpful gentleman in the tourism office was empathetic, but could do nothing to help us retrieve our card. We would have to come back Monday morning when the bank opened. Unfortunately, we were supposed to be in Rome on Monday morning, not Chiusi. Fortunately, we were in a rental car and could easily return to Chiusi on our way to Rome, not going too far out of our way. Our additional, post Chiusi, rules for ATM withdrawals:

1. Withdrawal from an ATM only during banking hours.
2. Withdrawal from ATMs in the town in which you are staying. If you are planning a daytrip, take plenty of cash.
3. Try not to transact business on the day prior to leaving town.

If you transact business via an ATM during banking hours, should a problem occur, you can possibly resolve the problem immediately. If it can't be resolved right away, the bank will at least be local when you have to return the next day. The last rule is the toughest. It's hard to figure out how much money you need and you are doing your best not to be caught with too much (or too little) cash in the local currency. But avoiding last day transactions allows time for working out a problem should it occur

End of story...We were able to obtain our ATM card Monday morning on the way to Rome. It was a stressful morning but everything ended well!

Another ATM rule adopted when we were down to one ATM card was, when possible, obtain cash on a separate outing. If an ATM is not far from your accommodation, run out, get your cash, and then return home. This way you don't have to carry your ATM card with you all day. In addition, any extra cash you obtained can be left behind as well.

When you have Internet access, check your bank account within twenty-four hours of an ATM withdrawal. Not only will you see the exchange rate you obtained for the withdrawal, you can also see if the correct amount of money was debited from your account. If there is a problem, you can go to the bank and attempt to correct it. In Moshi, Tanzania, an ATM withdrawal left me with a returned card but no cash. When we checked our bank account, it turned out money had been deducted from our account for that same exact transaction. We went back to the bank and they tracked down the problem. They concurred with our conclusion, but somehow, our account was never credited back for the fumbled transaction. After leaving town we continued to try to correct this error via email but still had no luck.

Use guidebooks and other travelers' information to discover "quirks" regarding restrictions, limitations or strange practices that might affect your ability to obtain cash. We had read that Luang Prabang, Laos had no ATM machines. Along the way we confirmed that this information was dated and that they now have two ATM machines in town. Still a little insecure with the information, we obtained extra Thai Bhat we could exchange in a Laos bank if necessary. We were able to obtain Laos Kip at an ATM so we used our extra Thai Bhat upon our return to Thailand. Another quirk we had heard was that the ATM in the

Buenos Aires airport would restrict your cash withdrawal to one hundred Argentinean Pesos per transaction or the equivalent of about $82 US. Even with two cards, we weren't able to get anywhere near enough money to pay for our apartment upfront. This caused a bit of a problem with our landlord but we were able to obtain plenty of cash the next day at an ATM machine in town. And the weirdest story comes from Rapa Nui. I had read that there was only one ATM on the island and that the machine would only work with an ATM card affiliated with MasterCard; ours were affiliated with VISA. Marty thought this bizarre and felt it couldn't possibly be true but I wasn't taking any chances. Our last day in Tahiti, we ran around to multiple ATM machines, at various banks, in order to obtain a large amount of cash – here too each ATM machine restricted your cash withdrawal. At the airport, we took our French Polynesian Francs and converted them to US dollars. We arrived in Rapi Nui to discover that everything that I had read was true. We were totally unable to use the ATM machine. Had we not obtained the extra cash in Tahiti, we would have had a major problem.

Notify your bank and credit card companies of what you are about to embark upon. If you live in Madison, WI and all of a sudden there is a VISA charge or ATM transaction in Montevideo, Uruguay, they might find that suspicious and freeze your card until they can verify that it is not a fraudulent transaction. If they freeze your card, you will be unable to use it until you get the matter cleared up. This could take days! The longer you are on the road, the greater the chance this will happen as they will see transactions hopping from one country to another. Outline which countries you will be in and when and make it clear you do not want transactions from these countries viewed as fraudulent.

We left home with about $2500 in US dollars for use when dollars were necessary. This currency should be in new or nearly new bills and nothing larger than a $20. You would be surprised by not only how much US dollars are desired, but how often they are <u>needed</u> to obtain something. And, when they are needed, they want new and small bills! The number one thing we needed US dollars for was on the spot visas.

You can obtain US dollars on the road as we did in Tahiti, but there is a cost. First you withdraw money from the ATM machine in the local currency. Even without an ATM charge, you lose money on the currency exchange. Once you have local currency, you can then take it to the bank for conversion into US dollars. Of course, for the privilege of converting your money back into US dollars, there is another exchange rate loss and sometimes even a commission. Having US dollars in your original stash can save you money and hassle for those times when you will need it.

We also had 5000 Euros in our pocket when we left the US. Over the course of the last year of planning, the US dollar was sinking relative to the Euro. Since our first three months of travel would be spent in Europe, we were desperately hoping the trend would reverse. When it was clear the Euro was doing nothing but getting stronger, we decided to cut our losses and buy Euros while still here in the US. It turned out to be a good move but was only feasible because we were going to Europe first. If you are thinking about doing something like this, take into account the practicality of it all. It can't just be about the cost savings. Also, be aware that no one will want large bills so you need to try to obtain smaller bills if you make an exchange.

On travel days you will need to carry everything, but when you are out on a day to day basis, be selective as to what you carry. You may be used to carrying a wallet which holds all your "cash and cards," but remember, Dorothy, you are not in Kansas anymore. Carry only the amount of foreign currency you think you will need for the day and leave the rest at your accommodation in a safe place. If you don't anticipate needing your credit cards or ATM card, leave those behind as well, or maybe just carry one credit card with you. If your wallet, backpack, money belt etc. is either lost or stolen, you lose only what you've carried that day.

Regardless of how diligent you were at taking care of everything you left behind, there will be financial issues that crop up. A bill that gets mailed versus e-billed, an unexpected IRS request for past taxes (are any IRS notices really expected???), a check received for an inheritance from a long lost aunt who died. The person handling your mail should either have access to your checking account or have a stash of cash from which they can draw to pay these unexpected bills. Before leaving, I left my sister Donna (our mail guardian) with $1000 which she deposited into her checking account. Whenever a bill arrived in the mail, she would email me to ask what she should do about it.

If it was legitimate, I would have her pay the bill. She was to keep a record of what was spent and then reimburse us upon our return for any unused portion. I assumed she would have money left, but, as it turns out, about eight months into the trip, I needed to send her another check. I also left Donna a stash of deposit slips for our checking account. Occasionally, but not nearly often enough, she would receive a check in the mail which she could deposit directly into our account.

In order to be able to transact your business, you need to know the myriad of user names and passwords you established for all your different accounts. It's best to vary these from account to account and not use the same one across the board. This means a lot of user names and passwords! We carried a small notebook containing all the needed information, being as cryptic as possible when writing these passwords down. Our "little purple notebook" contained lots of other valuable and useful information: card numbers for each of our credit cards as well as phone numbers to call for customer assistance (these came in handy when Marty's wallet was stolen with all of his credit cards), frequent flyer numbers, social security numbers (if you are traveling with kids and don't know their numbers), bank account numbers and bank and investment company contact information. Make sure the contact numbers you have are for international calls. The book also contained addresses and phone numbers for friends and family and people who we hired to take care of things around the house. Any information you might want to get your hands on quickly (without having computer access) could be written in this book for easy reference.

Finances Buenos Aires Style...

Wednesday, April 15, 2009
RIPPED OFF...TWICE!
Posted by Marty at 7:29 AM

We were on the subway heading back from the artisan market near the Recoleta Cemetario when we noticed a person acting weird. He was three feet away, acting like he was getting out of the subway car...on the wrong side. He dropped some coins and scurried to look for them. In an instant, he was out of the subway car, on the correct side. Weird. I didn't realize how weird until we started out the next morning. I asked lisa "Have you seen my wallet?" We looked all over and realized that the "strange guy" on the subway was just a diversion and someone else had stuck their hand in my pocket and extracted my wallet. There was the initial shock. There was the anger. There was this feeling of "how stupid can you be"....carrying all your credit cards when you seldom use them...or having my ATM card with me all the time, even though we don't need money...or...just something else that I could have prevented. I was in a daze for a couple of hours. My steadfast mate lisa, always thinking, called Nathan, my brother-in-law on Skype and he then dialed the credit card companies which allowed lisa to talk to them to cancel the cards. When I returned with a fresh supply of Argentinean pesos, compliments of lisa's account (and her ATM card), I finished the calls with the help of Nathan. THANKS NATHAN!!!!!!!!!!!!!!!!!!!!!!!!!!!!!!!!!!!!!

Everything is now OK. Credit cards cancelled. ATM card cancelled. lisa had all the numbers we needed to call in case this sort of thing happened written down in a separate book. I lost about $60-80 US and the morning we spent cancelling all the cards could have been spent doing something else. And I lost the nice wallet I bought from the Bangkok wallet guy for $5.75. Damn!

Now I really need to get it out, to journal about this, even if it's in a blog. I was ripped off AGAIN in the subway today. I had maybe 400 pesos on me (estimate about $110.00 US) in large bills in one pocket and all my small stuff in another pocket. The train was extremely crowded with people squeezing in to get on the subway. I'm holding on to Siena with one hand and grasping (protecting) my backpack with the other. I didn't have a handhold so I was held up by the other people around me. Someone raises my outer right pocket and lifts the money. I didn't feel it happen. Apparently you seldom do.

When I discover the loss, I am stunned. How could this happen again? Deep in my subconscious I knew the rip off of my wallet earlier was a once in a lifetime occurrence, not something that is going to happen again three days later. I feel victimized by just being a tourist. I feel that people here are out to rip you off. Who can I trust? This has caused me to want to get on the subway and yell "HERE I AM. AN AMERICAN. A TOURIST. COME GET ME. COME TAKE MY MONEY. Would people just think I am crazy? Or would they in some small way be embarrassed for how "unsafe" their city, country and perhaps their continent is? On the other hand, New York isn't safe. Over-the-Rhine in Cincinnati isn't safe. So why should a very busy, crowded part of a South American city of fifteen million people be safe? I don't know. It just should.

I'm naïve. Even after ten months plus on the road, I still am. I'm still a little kid from Morganfield in Western Kentucky where you say HI to everyone and don't lock your house (even on vacation). Must I be callous and non- trusting or am I the fool? A fool for not wearing the money belt? A fool for just not knowing better? OK Marty, enough moaning. Grow up!! I must find a way to protect myself, my family and my possessions. This isn't Oz, it's a crime possible (I almost said crime ridden but that's a big overstatement) city. Was it only in America in 1965 when people would return a wallet with the money still in it? Maybe. Will this have a lasting impact on me? Probably not. I'll wear the money belt for awhile, at least until we get to Florida. I'll be extra vigilant, but probably only till we get home. I don't want to be paranoid. I want to trust my fellow man, whether they are white, black, red, American, Chinese, Indian and yes, Argentinean.

Chapter Seventeen

HOBBIES FOR THE ROAD AND DOWN DAYS

When you go on vacation you take a book - a guide book or maybe a novel. Possibly you're a periodical reader and take a magazine or two. You read on the plane, in the car (assuming you don't get car sick) or on the beach. If you're an avid reader, you might take several books. That works for a one or two week vacation, but we're talking the big time now. It's not what are you going to do on the plane ride, it's what are you going to do on the 32 plane rides, 9 train trips, 4 ferry crossings, in the evenings and on "down days," for the next year!

Living life on the road, you have to think about how you are going to spend your "relaxation" time. You can't be on the go 100% of the time, it would be exhausting. You'll need a break; everyone will need a break. But you don't want to be sitting there "twiddling your thumbs." How are you going to occupy your time?

We gave this question some thought before we left and in all honesty, we didn't have a lot of answers. We left the US with the bare minimum of things to occupy our time: books, journals, schoolwork, playing cards, dice, scissors, glue sticks, art supplies and a computer. The rest we figured out along the way.

Books

We're a big reading family so books were an issue. Plus, we have two school aged children who were supposed to be getting an education while on the road. We stocked up at the local library sale, buying only used paperbacks. Friends donated books, knowing they would never see them again. We only packed books that at least two people were willing to read. That way we'd get double duty out of each book we hauled. Sometimes it was a book all four of us would enjoy. The original plan was for each person to pack two or three books in their bag. But after packing, we had additional room so more books went in. Since they were items that would get "used up" and discarded, having extra books was not going to be a long term problem.

There was no way we could carry enough books for a year. I looked into shipping books to various locations, but it was costly. A cheaper option was "special delivery." My mother was coming to meet us in Poland one month into the trip. We gave her a small stack of books to bring with her. It was no big deal. She knew she would have to leave extra room in her suitcase for souvenirs anyway, so why not use that extra room on her outbound trip for our books. If someone is planning on visiting you along the way, ask them if they would consider bringing you books.

Other than the books my mother brought us, we were on our own. Sources for reading materials were varied: other travelers, book exchanges in shops or hostels, English language bookstores, bookshelves in the apartments we stayed in. You don't get to read the latest New York Times Bestsellers or books you've wanted to read for years, but you do discover all kinds of new books that you may not have read otherwise as well as encounter some interesting people and places along the way.

Some great trip memories are of books we read and how we obtained them. Siena was out of reading material in Ljubljana, Slovenia. We were replacing a lost water bottle in an outdoor store which happened to have a book exchange. There we picked up a copy of Dune - House Atreides. She knew nothing about it but was willing to give it a try. She read it and loved it. Then Avocet read it and loved it. Then Marty read it and loved it. From that point forward, anytime we were in a used bookshop or at a book exchange, we looked for the sequels. The second in the series was obtained at a used book stall at Salamanca Market in Hobart, Tasmania, and the third in the series was discovered at a used English Language bookshop in Buenos Aires. At the end of our stay in Buenos Aires, we went back to Walrus Books and were able to purchase a three book set of Dune books to continue the series.

We were able to find books for the entire year using these sources. We always left finished books behind and carried only those still to be read – sometimes carrying more books than desired if we made a good find. We never bought new books which were costly, even in English speaking countries. The one exception to the new book rule was made in India, where new English Language books are downright cheap.

Journals

You will probably want to document your journey. We each left home with a notebook and a set of pens and pencils in our backpacks. The notebooks were nothing fancy, strictly functional. The pens, ordinary, but ones with waterproof and fade proof ink. We journaled on a regular basis – some of us everyday, others, skipping a day or two but always keeping them up to date. When the notebooks ran out, we purchased new ones. In India, we picked up beautiful handmade paper journals for less than what our original notebooks cost. In the end, each of us had two or three journals with a year's worth of memories to read and reread over time. When we traveled, we always carried our journals in our backpacks, never in our checked luggage – taking no risk of losing them. For the same reason, we opted to never mail home our completed journals. Mailing them home or carrying them in checked luggage would have lightened our load, but the emotional loss of missing our journals was not worth the trade off for a lighter backpack.

Marty's journal was writing only, but the girls and I embellished ours with collaging. Using the scissors and glue sticks we brought, we inserted into our journals ticket stubs, pictures, cut outs from brochures, matchbook covers, etc. Avocet got so into collaging we bought her a separate notebook she could use for her masterpieces.

Playing Cards, Dice and other Games

We had two decks of regular playing cards and a specialized card game. In addition, we had a set of dice for an assortment of dice games. All of these are small, easy to carry and can be used by the group or individually. We didn't use them as much as we thought we would. We imagined our family, after a day out exploring Auckland, New Zealand, sitting around, enjoying family time with a deck of cards. That's a perfect scenario when Mom and Dad have been at work all week, the kids in school, and you need to reconnect. But when you are with each other twenty-four hours a day, seven days a week, you are so immersed in family time that by the end of the day, you want some space. Siena and Avocet played with all of these - they were well worth bringing.

We played verbal games a lot. That's because you can play them anywhere: waiting in line to check in at the airport, sitting in a restaurant waiting for food, on a long train ride... We started off with a game friends at home had taught us called The Made Up Word Game. One person sets parameters (up to three): number of syllables, beginning letter, ending letter, contains a specific letter. The player then invents a word using the given parameters. All others playing then make up a definition for the "word". The person who made up the word picks the definition that she likes best.

Soon we got bored with that game so we made up others. We played our own version of Jeopardy using our travel information for category ideas. Quito, Ecuador Trivia for $300 anyone? We also invented games rooted in our travel experiences. What did we all eat in a particular restaurant? Favorite meals of the trip. Favorite activities of the trip. Most memorable scenery. These games were not only a fun way to pass the time, they also helped reinforce the memories we were creating as a family.

Art Supplies

None of us are artists, (Marty might disagree) though some are better than others (I am not one of the better ones). But drawing or painting is not only a good way to pass the time, it is a different way to experience a sight. I packed one artist drawing pad, a good box of colored pencils with a sharpener and a small watercolor set with extra brushes. None of this took much room. Occasionally we would go out armed with our art supplies, pick a scenic spot, and draw. The end results were cut and pasted into our journals, or kept on the art pad for future use. One time, in Hobart, Tasmania, Siena and Avocet, feeling particularly inspired, spent hours drawing in our apartment with an entire portfolio to show for their efforts.

Needlework

Crocheting and knitting would be great hobbies for the road but none of us knew how. I used to crochet but it's been years and I've never passed it on to my children. Once on the road, finding someone to teach us, in English, was impossible, until we hit Christchurch, New Zealand. At the weekend market, we purchased a knitting loom. This was a piece of wood with nails that looks like a variation of spool knitting. We bought one for the girls and later picked up yarn. First the girls knitted a small scarf for one of their dolls. With a success under their belt, Siena knitted herself a full sized scarf (her "bufunda," scarf in Spanish) which she wore on the chilly Ecuadorian evenings. Avocet's scarf is in process and will hopefully be finished by winter.

I had thought that knitting and/or crocheting would be a great hobby to take on the road and our experience confirmed this. The needles take up little space and you can get yarn anywhere in the world. The finished product can become part of your wardrobe or given as gifts to friends you make along the way. Remember when you fly that those knitting needles need to be in your checked luggage or you will lose them to airport security.

Computer

The hobbies we could never think of at home were born on the road out of our desire to document our trip and to stay in touch with friends and family. We had always planned on keeping a blog, but by having our own computer, we were able to blog more frequently, more extensively, any time, day or night. When we didn't have an Internet connection, we wrote blogs on Word, later uploading it to Blogger. We kept everyone at home informed of what we were up to, but more importantly, this became the family's documentation of our adventure. If someone felt particularly passionate about a specific subject matter, they were the one who got to write that blog. Sometimes we would have to negotiate who got what. It was a great writing curriculum for Siena and Avocet. We posted 240 blogs over the course of our trip. Check it out at: Oneworldonetrip.blogspot.com.

Our blog wasn't the only way of keeping folks back home informed. In the quiet of the evening or on a "down day," Marty or I would go through our pictures, picking and choosing which to keep and which to delete. Once culled, we edited, titled and shared them with those on our picture update list. This was a huge task, taking a considerable amount of time. Before we left, we would never have thought of picture maintenance as a hobby, but it certainly became one.

Once we decided to take a computer with us, I thought this would be a great opportunity for everyone to learn how to type properly. I had taken typing in high school so I was a speed typist from way back. Marty was a hunt and peck type of guy and the girls knew the concept of proper typing but had never really practiced it. I ordered a typing program and loaded it onto the computer. Siena and Avocet had the opportunity to use the program about a dozen times before we lost it in our computer crash in Poland. We didn't bring the disk with us to reinstall the program; you, however, should! The good news was that a dozen times was enough for the girls to get the idea. They are now speed typists just like their Mom. Dad, on the other hand, will be a hunt and peck kind of guy the rest of his life.

Emails are a way to have basic communication with people you know, but they can also become a hobby, a subset of the dying art of letter writing. It doesn't involve beautiful stationary, wonderful penmanship, a pretty stamp and the excitement of receiving something in the mailbox, but it is a way to communicate with friends and family. I'm not talking about the one paragraph emails to pass on some information or the forwards that go around the world and back. I'm talking about serious letter writing. Over the year, I kept in touch with six friends back home with this type of writing and I never felt as close to those friends as I did from 12,000 miles away.

Our computer was an activity source on the road. Marty followed his favorite sports teams as if he were still in the US. The girls logged on to their favorite websites and played games. We rented movies (or purchased pirated ones on the streets) and had family movie nights. Occasionally we had a music night, logging onto YouTube and taking turns picking out songs to enjoy. Be forewarned about this one. One night during dinner in Auckland, New Zealand we "YouTubed." It turned out that unlimited Internet was not exactly unlimited and we got an Internet bill $45.00 in excess of the standard charge. Expensive meal! Thank goodness there was a good exchange rate in New Zealand at the time.

The computer was one of our prized possessions and I wouldn't do a trip without it. But if screen time is an issue with your family, make sure you set clear rules about usage time and place. For the most part, we did not have issues till the end. The girls wanted to go home and preferred computer time to going out and doing something. At that point, we had to set up some guidelines and limitations.

Down Days

"Down Day" is the term we used when having a day with nothing in particular going on. Sometimes down days were scheduled in between active, busy days, and sometimes, down days were forced upon us, when we were all just too tired to motivate ourselves. Down days are a must. And we enjoyed them. It gave us time to do all of our "life stuff", as well as our "hobbies." They gave us an opportunity to reinvigorate ourselves. On down days we could sleep a little later, pick up something special for breakfast, take a nap in the middle of the afternoon or just go for a walk. If there was a rainy day in the forecast, we would try to plan a "down day" – sometimes it would work out and other times, we would need a down day before that rainy day ever rolled around. Now, back at home, I could really use a down day!

This Was Written on a Down Day...

Sunday, January 18, 2009
SAME SAME BUT DIFFERENT
Posted by lisa at 5:15 AM

After seven months of traveling, we are now finally in the Land Down Under - Australia. In our minds, it was going to be kind of like being back in the US for a while, just the Southern Hemisphere version of it. This is not necessarily true. Yes, there are similarities, but also differences; and there are expectations unmet...

1. We both speak English, kinda sorta. We often have to ask people to repeat themselves, spell something out, or we just smile and walk away, asking each other, did anyone understand what they said? Often this is no different than when we would be in a non-English speaking country and the person who we were speaking to would speak English to us.

2. We use the dollar and they use the dollar. Part of a dollar is called cents in both places. It only cost $ .70 US to buy $1.00 Australian - we like that! It does however, take $2.50 Australian to buy an "American Candy Bar" - we don't like that.

3. We drive on the right side of the road, the Aussies drive on the wrong side; oops, I mean the left side. This requires you to look right first when crossing the street and it also means that on walkways, stairs and escalators, people hang to the left just like the traffic patterns.

4. All of their food products have nutritional labeling just like at home, however, they don't have a line for calories but

instead have one for energy. Since I'm always looking for more energy, this works for me!

5. The ADA, American Disabilities Act, must have conveyed to the Australian Disabilities Act for this is the first country that we have been to in our seven months of travels that has cared for their citizens with disabilities to the extent that the US has. Clearly, traveling here with a physical disability would be much easier than any of the other countries that we have been to on this trip.

6. Sydney is an international city and has people of all nationalities living here. Just like in the US, if you see someone who is Asian, Hispanic, Black, Indian etc. it doesn't mean they are tourists; here in Sydney, there's a good chance they are Australians.

7. Public transportation is for everyone, regardless of the time of day or the route, the buses are filled with people. In the US, in most cities, public transportation is for the poor i.e. for those who can't afford cars.

8. Once we decided to take along a computer, we were curious as to where we would have Internet access in our accommodations and where we wouldn't. Certain places were obvious: Tanzania – no, India – no, Thailand – no, European countries – yes, Australia – yes. Well, we have had Internet access almost everywhere so far, but here we are, in Australia, and this blog is being written at the local Internet cafe. Go figure. Expectations are just another word for premeditated frustrations!

We thought about how easy things would be once we reached Australia. Some things are easier, but some things are not.

We are still travelers in a foreign land and with that come challenges regardless of where you go. Then again, we have challenges when at home too, just different.

Chapter Eighteen

WHEN WE WEREN'T DOING LAUNDRY

With 358 days of traveling, they couldn't all be "Down Days," "Travel Days" or days filled with "Life Stuff." So what were we doing the rest of the time? We were out exploring the world: climbing to the top of the Leaning Tower of Pisa, walking down the streets of Moshi, Tanzania observing the locals at work, trekking the Andes Mountains in Chile.

On "Out Days," we would don our day pack and go forth. Typically one day pack would suffice, occasionally two were required. The day pack would be loaded with the following items:

Map
Our notes on the locality
Multiple bottles of water
Snacks
Sunscreen
Hand sanitizer
Lip balm
Pen and/or pencil
Chewing gum
Change for public transportation
Rain jackets
Toilet paper (in a plastic bag)

Day to day activities weren't something we planned in advance, but most often when we set out for the day, we knew where we were going, how to get there and what we were going to do. We still left room for spontaneity and for days where we would just wander.

Activities on the road have a different look, a different feel. When you're in another culture, just observing life is an activity. Getting lost provides hours of entertainment and possibly an exciting adventure. Doing something as simple as going to the zoo becomes an ethnic experience. And shopping offers a lifetime of memories.

In Moshi, Tanzania where "sidewalk" seamstresses line the streets, we decided to employ one to make outfits for Siena and Avocet. The girls picked out material from her selection of fabrics then drew what they wanted in the woman's notepad. After making some adjustments to their drawings, the woman proceeded to measure the kids. Seeing this, I wanted to have something made as well, but didn't like her selection of fabrics. Several local English speaking onlookers explained to me that there were multiple fabric shops close by. The next thing I knew, we had a lively entourage following us through town looking for fabric. Our purchase of a few dresses turned into an event with clothing and cool memories for souvenirs.

When exploring an area, look past the obvious; look for things that are new and different. Rick Steves calls this exploring "Through the back door." In Thailand, don't just visit the Wats (Buddhist Temples) but go to a Monk Chat where you can find out more about Buddhism by asking a monk questions. They get to practice their English while you get a religion lesson. Attend a meditation class or take part in a Buddhist ritual (making sure you first know all the rules so you don't offend someone). Don't just eat the food, take a cooking class and learn how to make it.

Knowing we would be in South American Spanish speaking countries for three months, we decided to learn Spanish. Prior to arriving in Chillan, Chile, Marty contacted the friends we would be visiting, and asked Luz if she would tutor our family in Spanish. We continued our Spanish studies in Valpariso, Chile and in Buenos Aires, Argentina. Marty found Pamela in Valpariso via Craigslist.org and Paz in Buenos Aires via TripAdvisor.com. All three teachers offered opportunities to delve further into the culture and we really learned the language.

Our explorations took us to the obvious as well as the obscure, and we were always surprised by what captured our interest; not always what we thought it would be. We had multiple discussions about expectations and disappointments.

158

When We Weren't Doing Laundry

The sights, activities and locations we most looked forward to, often provided the greatest disappointments. Maybe it's impossible for things to live up to the expectations we create for them. We were all anxious as we wound our way through the Vatican Museum to get to the end to see the Sistine Chapel. When we arrived the kids said "Is this it?" The disappointment was written all over their face and reflected back to them from mine. A tuk tuk ride from Luang Prabang, Laos, however, placed us at Kuang Si Falls, probably the most beautiful waterfall I have every seen, totally unexpected.

Despite attempts to have unique experiences, we still suffered from travel saturation. We weren't tired of being on the road, we just felt numb to many of the new sights. We were are no longer in awe of the world's treasures but merely taking them in. As I became aware of this, I felt sad that I wasn't fully appreciating all we were doing. I'm starting to come to the conclusion that this is our mind's way of handling the overload. Now back at home, I find myself reliving those moments with an appreciation I didn't have at the time.

Expectations are Premeditated Disappointments...

Monday, November 3, 2008
<u>FOOD, INDIA AND EXPECTATIONS</u>
Posted by lisa at 3:30 AM

If you follow our blog, you will remember that I was pretty rough on Italy with respect to food (see Food, Italy and Expectations in September's blogs). Hey, I was really anticipating some incredible food in Italy and felt disappointed that it didn't pan out. But that is old news at this point, now we are in India.

Our original thought was that we would eat our way through Europe and then lose all the weight we gained, in Africa and India - either because the food wouldn't be very good or because we were physically sick from traveling in third world countries. Now that we have traveled Africa and are 2/3 the way through India I am pleased to report that no one has gotten sick and that we are not losing any weight due to poor food. Just the opposite - the food is fantastic!

In Cincinnati we live in a neighborhood where we can walk to our choice of three different Indian restaurants (all Northern Indian). Sophia (one of our faithful blog followers) asked if the food was just like Ambar, one of these Indian restaurants. Sophia, the answer is yes, just like Ambar - only better, greater variety and CHEAPER! You can get all your Indian favorites here: Masala, Paneer, Tandori Chicken, Butter Chicken, Biryani and of course all the wonderful Indian breads. The same dish can vary greatly from one restaurant to the next but for the most part, they are all great. The only thing I don't like is that a lot of times, your rice will not be hot, just room temperature. At home a piece of plain Naan is about $2.00 if I remember correctly, here it

160

is $.30. A dish of Saag Paneer at home will set you back about $8.00 but here, in a nice restaurant, it will cost you about $.90. We often find ourselves ordering excess food just so we can try something new and figure, what the heck, it's only another dollar! Here a family of 4 can eat for 300 Rupees ($6.00), the price of one Coke in Venice.

When we were north in Mcleodganj, we had the option of not only eating the wonderful Indian food, but also Tibetan food. After a while we gave up on the Indian food figuring that we could get that when we reached Jaipur, so in Mcleodganj we ate Tibetan. That was equally wonderful. Avocet and Siena discovered Momos, dumplings filled with potatoes and cheese, or vegetables or lamb. Those are the three most popular fillings but there are others. They have incredible noodle soups like Thankthuk with flavorful broths, vegetables, noodles and your choice of meat (other than beef) if you choose. It's a meal in itself. The noodle dish Chitsu was one of my favorites. We made sure to return to one of our favorite Tibetan restaurants the day we were leaving to get our last fix.

If you are willing to risk it, you can eat street food for less than $.50 and it looks and smells awesome. So far we haven't been willing to take that risk and content ourselves with the smells as we go by. Now the only thing I need to figure out is where I'm going to lose those extra pounds that I thought would be taken care of here in India!

Chapter Nineteen

THE PEOPLE CONNECTION

When traveling, you "connect with people" in different ways:

> ➤ Friends or family who visit you from home
> ➤ Local residents referred by friends or family
> ➤ Fellow travelers you meet along the way
> ➤ Fellow travelers whose paths you cross again

Each option presents wonderful opportunities, but also potential issues worth consideration.

It's important for you and your travel companions to bond together and establish your all important travel routine. To do this, you need to be alone as a family or a couple. Entertaining long term visitors during the early parts of your travel itinerary will prevent you from doing this. We started off with a three week stay in Haarlem, The Netherlands. While several requests were made to visit us there, we declined them all, instead inviting them to join us further along our journey. This gave our family the full three weeks to bond together, establish a routine and get used to being away from home and being on the road together.

Faces from Home

Longer term visits will be friends or family coming from home. Having traveled a long way, they will want to stay awhile. But even visits from the best of friends can quickly get old. Keep your visits down to a week for the best of relations and shorter for others. They can visit the rest of Argentina on their own.

The People Connection

Take into consideration when planning for a visit:

> - Where are they going to stay? Are they expecting to stay with you? If not, where? Is that convenient?
> - How independent of a traveler are they? Will they go out on their own? Or will they expect you to be their tour guide?
> - Do you share similar interests or will you want to do different things? How will you work out those differences?
> - Are there physical limitations to consider? Can they walk as much as you? Climb stairs? Climb mountains? Are they going to hold you back from doing things you want to do? Are you going to hold them back from doing things they want to do?
> - What is their financial situation relative to yours? Will they be looking to eat in four star restaurants while you're on a budget? Will you be looking to go to an expensive museum while they're looking for the "free day" at another?
> - Is one of you traveling with children while the other is looking for adult time?

There is room for lots of potential conflict when even your closest friends come to visit. Looking at these in advance and working through them can better assure you a good time and even save your relationship.

One month into our trip, my mother came to visit us for a week in Krakow, Poland. We all love my mother dearly and get along well. Still, it was an interruption to our family's routine. Knowing her physical limitations and her interests, we planned our three week visit in Krakow with this in mind. We visited the salt mine with hundreds of stairs, before she arrived. The long bus ride to Zakopane in the Tatra Mountains where we would walk long distances and riding bikes along the Vistula River were also done before she came. But the horse drawn carriage ride the kids were dying to take and the day trip to Auschwitz were reserved for Bubie's (Grandma's) visit as these were appropriate activities for her physical condition and interests.

Connecting With Friends or Family on Location

"You're going to Slovenia; I know someone who lives there!" "My penpal from fourth grade lives in Auckland, you should look her up while you're in New Zealand." "My second cousin once removed lives somewhere in The Netherlands, here's her email"...

Once you announce your itinerary, many will know somebody somewhere for you to meet. When you connect with someone in their own city, it's much less complicated. You don't have the same issues as when someone comes to visit you. If it's very important to meet these people, let them know in advance when you plan to arrive. It would be sad to go half way around the world, only to discover once you got there, they're away on a business trip that could have been rescheduled. If sharing time with the referred person is of minor interest, wait until your arrival, or shortly before, to contact them.

Contacting someone you don't know, a friend's distant cousin, can feel awkward. My advice, push through the awkwardness and just do it! When you are a stranger in a strange land, having access to a local can be wonderful. Contact in advance allows them to make itinerary or sight seeing suggestions. They might offer their services as a local guide for a day, or send you in the direction of the best restaurant in town for local food. In countries where there's a language barrier, an English speaking local gives you the opportunity to ask questions and have discussions you might not otherwise have. And, it's always a delight to just meet new people.

If you are travelling with children and can share time with another family, it gives your children much needed "kid time." It's also an opportunity for a cultural exchange that no day of sightseeing is going to offer. Even if the other kids speak a limited amount (or no) English, they find a way to play together. If the people who you are meeting don't have children, remember that what might interest you, may bore your children. Select a park or playground as a meeting spot so your children can be entertained while you enjoy your visit. If that's not possible, be sure your kids have some form of activity with them: books, magazines, cards, etc.

Once settled into our apartment in Haarlem, I emailed the cousin of a friend. Via email, we made a plan to meet at

Linneaushof, Europe's Largest Playground. Carol and her two children spent the entire day with us. Siena and Avocet had a blast playing with Carol's kids in a unique environment we probably would otherwise have not visited. Carol, Marty and I spent the day talking. After the usual introductory discussions, we moved on to the economics of Holland, the work system, the school system and the behavioral habits of the Dutch kids at the park. We parted leaving Carol with our email and blog addresses, occasionally hearing from her throughout our trip.

In Ljubljana, Slovenia, we made time to visit Natasa and Alenka. Friends of mine had previously met the two sisters while traveling in South America and passed along their names. They picked us up at the bus station near their town and had us to their family home where we met their young children and parents. We shared a meal, drinking wine made from the grapes grown in the family vineyard. Marty and I had a lovely time, our girls, however, were bored – we hadn't been prepared!

We then invited Natasa and Alenka to dinner. They came into the city, joined us for a meal at a nearby restaurant, then to our apartment for dessert. This time we were prepared with a DVD rental from the local video store. Siena and Avocet took their leave, went to their room and watched Crocodile Dundee on the laptop. For the adults, the conversation never stopped. We learned that Slovenes get one year of paid maternity leave, extra vacation pay, three Euros each day for lunch (or lunch provided at work) and get paid for their mileage to and from work. Salaries are low compared to the cost of living, and it's hard to make ends meet if only one parent works. We talked about the history of Slovenia and the good living conditions under Tito in the former Yugoslavia. We discovered that people there want bigger and fancier cars just like in the US. We discussed everything from school hours to the Balkan War to Slovenian toilet paper. It was sad when the evening came to an end.

Meeting Fellow Travelers

These are the easiest social interactions; the spontaneous meetings that make traveling so exciting. They occur at bus stops, in parks, at Internet cafes, in restaurants... just about anywhere. Chances are, if you're a traveler, you enjoy these "friendships" as much as we do. They are great opportunities to have the desperately needed social experience outside of your travel companions. Lasting only an hour or sometimes all day, these connections are sources of information, of "Do's and "Don'ts" and serve as wonderful cultural exchanges. They require no planning, no forethought, no effort.

When meeting fellow travelers you will find people interested in what you are doing who want to check out your blog. By the time we reached Thailand, we had written our blog address on paper napkins, scrap pieces of paper, airline boarding passes and on people's hands. One day, in Chiang Mai, we passed a printer and came up with the "brilliant" idea of printing "business cards." We spent the rest of that afternoon and evening designing cards that included our first names, a logo, and our blog address. Sometimes, we wrote our email addresses on the back. We wished we had thought of the idea sooner!

Déjà Vu

Reconnecting with travelers you met previously on your journey is exciting; however, it's not quite as easy as when you met the first time. You have all moved on, are into the flow of a new country and are living with a different set of circumstances. It's still worth trying to get together if you can as it's great fun reconnecting with travelers.

In the town of Bagamoyo, about one hour north of Dar Es Salaam, Tanzania, we met a New Zealand couple who had moved their family to Dodoma, Tanzania where they were teaching at an English Language school. They were enjoying a week's vacation on the Indian Ocean and our families had a lovely time together. When we mentioned our plans to be in Auckland in February, we discovered that they would be there at the same time, taking a one month break from their post. We exchanged email addresses. Four months later and half a world away, we met again in their home in Auckland, sharing our travel stories as they talked about life in Dodoma and the progress of their school. The kids played and played. We shared a meal at their home before parting again

At the Mut Mee Guest House in Nong Khai, Thailand, we met many long term travelers. Unfortunately, our future paths did not cross with most, but with one crazy French couple, our paths would cross multiple times. Our itineraries were so similar that we would arrive and depart the same cities three or four times, always on the same day! We departed Sydney the day they arrived. We arrived to Auckland the day they departed. In Tahiti, we visited at the airport for two hours between our arriving and their departing. Finally, in Buenos Aires, Argentina, Charlotte and Erwan's itinerary overlapped ours for multiple days. With a large apartment at our disposal, we invited them to dinner, enjoyed an evening of food and wine, and had them stay overnight. Our one and only sleepover for the trip! The next day we toured the famous Recoleta Cemetery together, stopping for a drink before heading our separate ways. Two days later we had them back to our apartment for dinner and then went to a Tango Show. We said our final good-byes on Avenida 9 de Julio, our future itineraries heading in different directions.

Visiting Friends from Home in Their Native Home...

Tuesday, March 31, 2009
FELIZ CUMPLEANOS LUZ ELIANA

Posted by lisa at 8:15 AM

While our trip to Chillan hadn't been planned to coincide with Luz Eliana's birthday, our timing could not have been any better. A week after our arrival, we found ourselves trotting out to Luz's childhood home in San Nicholas to celebrate her birthday. Family (lots of it since Luz has four brothers and three sisters) and friends gathered for the festivities.

What transpired over the next seven hours is hard to describe. We felt like we were in a movie of Chile in days gone by. Vegetables were growing in the yard, grapes were hanging from their vines up above and chickens were roaming everywhere. We met so many people, it was hard to keep track of names or relationships. Almost no one spoke English and we know little Spanish but that didn't stop anyone from talking to us.

We helped Luz prepare a less than traditional pizza for dinner, which was cooked in a very traditional outdoor wood fired oven. Other foods served were more traditional. We cooked, we ate, we drank, we ate, we drank, we ate! Just when you thought the eating and drinking part was over, more people would show up and more food and wine would be served. Birthday cake topped off a great meal.

But the end of the meal didn't signify the end of the party! First there was a piñata to break open which Luz's mom succeeded in doing with her one and only blow. Candy spilled out everywhere and the kids (and Luz's mom) scampered around to quickly collect it. Next, the dancing. Luz's cousin Joel began a traditional Chilean "courting" dance (the "Cueca") while everyone stood around clapping out the beat. Almost everyone took a turn dancing – even us gringos, some doing better than others.

It was a wonderful evening filled with flavor; we all had such a great time! As we traveled the world over the past $9\frac{1}{2}$ months, we have had the opportunity to see so many amazing sights. But we never had the opportunity to share in someone's culture as intimately as we did on this night. Luz's Chilean birthday party will be something that we will remember for the rest of our lives and will certainly be one of the highlights of our year around the world.

Feliz cumpleanos Luz y muchas gracias!

And Visiting Natives in Their Home...

Monday, March 9, 2009
<u>FRIENDS IN FAR AWAY PLACES</u>
Posted by lisa at 4:36 AM

Back in the days when the world was a lot bigger, people actually wrote something called letters as a way of communicating with people in distant lands. And in an attempt to make the world seem a little bit smaller, fourth grade teachers encouraged students to get penpals from other English speaking countries to communicate with. My penpal, Lee from Australia, and I wrote for about two years and that was that. But my sister Donna and her penpal, Robyn from New Zealand, have been writing, emailing, Skyping and meeting/visiting each other for forty two years now. While Robyn has been to the US, Donna has not yet made it to New Zealand - but here I am!

Robyn has been a part of our family's life for a long time; not often in the foreground but never not in the background. When she came to the US twenty six years ago, she lived with Donna for about three months and was most definitely a part of the family. About eleven to twelve years ago, my parents had the opportunity to be in Auckland as part of an Australia and New Zealand tour and had a day with Robyn and by that time, her son Jeremy.

We met Robyn and Jeremy at Little Italy, a downtown restaurant, for dinner one night. A short evening, but that was OK, there was more to come. Saturday morning found the six of us wandering the streets of the Otara Polynesian Market. After several hours, we split up: Jeremy to connect with some of his friends, Marty and the girls to a museum, and Robyn and I to have a ladies' afternoon. What we did really wasn't important; it was just great to have five hours together to share our lives with each other.

On Sunday evening, we all went out to Robyn and Jeremy's house to have a BBQ where they shared their home, their hospitality and even some of their friends. It was a fun and enjoyable Kiwi night and certainly one of our New Zealand highlights.

Chapter Twenty

SOUVENIRS

For many, vacations mean shopping. It's a time when you're not burdened by day to day responsibilities, so you have more time to SHOP! Plus, there are awesome things to buy in many vacation destinations. As a long term traveler, you are not immune to this type of thinking, but, it won't play as big a role as you think. You will actually get tired of shopping. Browsing in unique markets around the world is fun; but after a while, it's just another market. Things look good on the streets but will it look as good in your house back home? Then there are budget considerations. You budgeted for six months of travel, not six months of shopping. You'll find yourself reining in the wallet and not splurging like you might were you on a two or three week vacation. You will buy things, just not as many as you imagine.

If you are traveling with kids, they will attempt to make up for your constraint. They are not thinking about budgets or where you are going to put this stuff while in transit or once you get home; they just see a lot of really cool stuff. And you, being the wonderful parent you are, will want them to have these mementos to remind them of this experience.

How did we deal with the souvenir issue? At home, we arranged for one of our friends to be our package guardian. This is not a difficult job so you should be able to get almost anyone who spends time at home (not traveling) to do it. Select someone who lives within driving distance, so when you return, picking up your packages is easy.

For Marty and I, choosing what to purchase came down to: How bad did we want it? Size? How long would we have to carry it prior to mailing it home? Would it look equally as good at home as it does here? Cost? In expensive countries (throughout Europe) there were few purchases made. Partly because of expense, but also because Westernized countries' "souvenirs" were not all that unique or interesting. Once we hit Africa and Asia, costs came down and the possibilities of uncommon mementos increased.

Fewer restrictions were placed on the kids. We still had to keep in mind the size and weight issues since we would be carrying it around then mailing it home. We wouldn't let them buy anything that couldn't fit into their suitcases or backpacks or made it too heavy to carry. We gave each of the girls a "country allowance." Every time we crossed into a new country, the girls each received the equivalent of $15 US, in local currency. This helped reduce the need of constantly saying "no." They had to make the decision whether or not they wanted that doll or this purse bad enough to part with some of their own money. We still bought them gifts, particularly traditional clothing items, and sometimes helped with purchases in the more expensive countries. Be prepared for arguments related to Hong Kong and China or Rapa Nui and Chile or any other country with nebulous borders.

We carried our souvenir and gift items around till we accumulated a significant mass. That could be months or merely weeks. It depended on what countries we were visiting, what types of gifts were available and what events took place in that time period. Avocet and Siena had a birthday in mid-November, increasing the gift haul substantially at that time. It required a shipment from Chiang Mai, Thailand. Marty's birthday, at the beginning of December, required another mailing just three weeks later from Luang Prabang, Laos. We had no mailing after that for another eight weeks.

Over the course of the year, we mailed home nine packages. If "By Sea" was an option, we chose that as it was cheaper and what was the hurry? We weren't going to be home anytime soon! Some countries no longer offer "By Sea" and only offer "Air Mail." It's quicker but more expensive. We mailed from some questionable locations like Moshi, Tanzania and Mcleodganj, India, but every single package arrived back in the US. The condition of the package was not always perfect and we had several damaged items, but all could be repaired with the exception of one poorly packaged painting mailed from Croatia.

Many post offices around the world sell packaging supplies like we do here. It makes preparing a package to ship easy and convenient. When it's not available, you scrounge around for a box and packing material as best you can. In Montepulciano, Italy, we created a sight rooting through grocery store dumpsters looking for the right size box. We gathered newspapers from recycling bins to use as packing material and purchased a roll of packing tape.

Our mailing experience in Mcleodganj, India was by far the most interesting. This is a small town, but they get a number of tourists as it is the exiled home of the Dalai Lama. We purchased a large number of textiles from one store and asked for a box in order to ship them. The shopkeeper instructed us to go to a stall near the post office. We set out, thinking we were going to this stall to purchase a box. It turns out this is the "packing" stall where you bring all your goods to be packed for mailing. With a sewing machine, cardboard and cloth, the gentleman proceeded to make us a "box" to ship our purchases. At the end of the process, he sewed a "pillowcase" from material and inserted the "box" into the "pillowcase." It was a work of art. We wrote our address on the "pillowcase" and took it next door to the post office for mailing.

Mailing the package was as much an experience as was the packing. Indians do not cue up like Americans or even like most Westerners. Given the hoards of people that live in India, they probably assume that if they were to cue up, it would never be their turn. They therefore push and shove until they get to the front of the line, including the monks! The post office in Mcleodganj was small, so the girls and I waited outside while Marty bravely entered. I watched through the open window as Indian after Indian went ahead of my all too polite husband. Other Westerners would come out and tell me that he will never survive in there. But India will get to even the most genteel southern gentleman and eventually I saw Marty extending his arms out making it difficult for anyone to pass. After this, each and every person that successfully passed him only served to make him more aggressive. An hour later, he emerged from the post office, cursing the cultural ways of India. Of course, now back at home, this is one of his favorite stories to tell.

What Will You be Buying?...

Friday, August 22, 2008
THE SHOPPING DIFFERENCE
Posted by lisa at 6:00 AM

Shopping is often a big part of people's vacations. Almost everyone shops at least for souvenirs, but often people shop for other items: new clothes or purse, local handicrafts or sometimes even big ticket items like jewelry. For some people, it's just a matter of having more time while on vacation to do something they are too busy to do otherwise. For others, it's just an enjoyable activity to include in their vacation plans.

When you are on the road for a year, shopping takes on a whole different meaning. For one thing, anything you buy, you will have to either cart around with you for another eleven months or ship home – have you seen shipping rates lately? For another thing, when you are on the road for this long, it is not a vacation, it is a way of life, and your shopping needs are different.

Instead of seeking out the local handicrafts, we spend time looking for stores that sell buttons so we can repair the few clothes that we brought with us. A new purse is not in order, but personal care products are. Now that we have been gone for eleven weeks, we are beginning to run out of our initial supplies. That may not seem like a big deal, but trust me, the products you are looking for are not necessarily sold in the same type of store you are used to buying them in. Toothpaste, sunscreen, body lotion and hair color (not that anyone around here uses that) are just a few of the items that we have had to search for. Also, making sure you end up

175

with the right item is important. My first attempt at body lotion produced body wash (as in soap) – try returning that product to the lady who only speaks Polish!

Then there's our big ticket item, English language books. We have found an English language bookstore in almost every city we have been in, but the books are outrageously priced. We are constantly on the lookout for used bookstores, book swaps and English speaking people who want to discard their books. So far we have acquired books in all those different ways. We have become scavengers when it comes to books and read what we can find which is not necessarily what we would have chosen. (Note: All four of us have discovered some great books this way)

Services are another thing that we have had to shop for. With short hair, I have my hair cut every six weeks. I had to find a salon in Krakow that I could trust to cut my hair and give me a good cut that would last until I have to seek someone out in Lucca, Italy who will do it again. (Africa is six weeks after that... yikes!) When my neck and shoulders were acting up, I had to find a massage therapist. Shopping for these services is as far as it gets from typical vacation shopping.

I see travelers in the food markets all the time buying fruit, yogurt, sandwiches, drinks and snack items. We too are buying all those, along with cereal, milk, wine, beer, spices, meats, butter, olive oil, rice, pasta, etc. We are not just picnicking, we are cooking and we have refrigeration.

Like many tourists we have bought some new clothes. There was a great second hand shop in Poland where everyone found something "new" to add to our tired wardrobe. And this past

Wednesday found us in Ljubljana's Central Market clothes stalls where we were trying to find Avocet some new pants as she is starting to outgrow the ones we brought on the trip. We were anticipating growth for the kids, just not this soon!

Siena and Avocet still hit the souvenir shops, but they are limited as to what they can buy both in terms of money and space and some places, like here in Slovenia, are just not set up for the tourist trade yet so the selection is very limited. It's all perspective. Some people get to come home with T-Shirts, we get to come home with Sonnen Milch (sun screen).

Chapter Twenty-One

EMOTIONAL ROLLER COASTER II

Now on the road, we're feeling a whole new set of emotions that, once again, we've deemed normal. We've settled into life as travelers. We no longer think about whether or not this is the craziest and most stupid thing we've ever thought about because we're doing it! We're no longer worried about whether or not everything will get done before we leave. We're gone! If it didn't get done before we left, oh well, it's too late now. And, we're no longer wondering if this is going to happen or if we are planning for the biggest letdown of our lives. It happened! We made it happen. And we're feeling the success of having turning a dream into a reality. Of course, that doesn't mean everything is peachy keen.

We have good days and bad days as we would were we back at home. Just because you're in Rome doesn't mean you can't have a bad day. Things often don't go as planned, therefore some days are filled with stress. Flights get changed (never for the better), hotels misplace your reservations and personal items get left behind leaving you scrambling.

It's not just the inconveniences of traveling that affect our mood and emotions. You know those days when kids wake up in the morning and say "I don't want to go to school today?" Well, now they wake up and say "I don't want to be traveling anymore." And some days we wake up saying the same exact thing. Traveling can become tiring. It's hard on the body and exhausting to the spirit. That's one of the reasons I recommend a slower pace and down days; it's a way to restore yourselves. But even with the slower pace and down days, we feel tired and sometimes wonder if we will make it through the rest of the year. We validate our children's feelings (and our own) and then brainstorm about what activity we can do in order to break the

178

mood. Sometimes it works but other times we have to just sit with the mood. New locations generate new interests; a change in culture brings about excitement and the feelings pass.

An unanticipated feeling that came up was boredom. We're traveling around the world, how can it be boring? Because at some point, like your routine at home, it just gets to be more of the same. The Saturday morning outdoor market in Harlem, The Netherlands was wonderful. We did almost all our grocery shopping there. It was such a nice change from shopping in an American style supermarket. But after a while, an outdoor market is just another outdoor market and it ceases to have the charm it had early on. Now it is a place to go food shopping. With similar sights and activities from one country to the next, there is a bit of a "been there, done that" feeling. We then try to find something totally different to do, something off the beaten path we have yet to experience: a cooking class, an adventure activity, biking to the next town, going out for tea, a weaving class.

An interesting downfall we experienced with long term travel was the jaded feeling that began to seep into our pores. Looking out over the vineyards of Tuscany was an incredible sight, but so was looking out over the Hong Kong Harbor and the view into the Ngorongoro Crater in Tanzania, and the foothills of the Himalayas in Mcleodganj, India. One incredible view after another gets to be just that, one incredible view after another. It's like too much of a good thing. When you see the world's best museums, shop in its most unique markets and see its top sights all in one trip, each individual sight begins to lose some of its splendor. We constantly reminded ourselves to appreciate each country for what it was and each sight for what it offered, without downgrading it because of what had come before.

Scared was a feeling that continued to rear its ugly head. Typically it appeared when we were about to leave one location to go to another. We arrived in a city knowing almost nothing: language, logistics, how public transportation worked, where the market was, how to use the washing machine. And then we learned it all and became comfortable and secure in our environment. Only to leave it all behind for the unknown of a new place, where we didn't know the language, the layout of the city, how public transportation worked... Often we wanted to stay in a city or town longer; I'm sure for that very reason.

Though the fearful feeling of changing venues never completely disappeared, I was aware that as time went on, the fear was lessening. Change was becoming a constant in our lives.

This Says it All...

Saturday, September 13, 2008
LIFE AT THREE MONTHS – A LITTLE JADED; A LITTLE WEARY
Posted by lisa at 3:40 AM

You know those fine dining restaurants you save for special occasions? You go there maybe two or three times a year for birthdays or anniversaries and really look forward to them. Imagine going three or four times a week. Would you continue to look forward to them? Would you savor them as much as you do when you only go a few times a year? That's a little bit how we are feeling at the moment - maybe a little too much fine dining! (Not literally) When you have a two week vacation that you have been looking forward to for a long time and you arrive in a beautiful city, you relish the site. When you arrive in a beautiful city after three months of one beautiful city after another, it feels a little bit like "just another beautiful city." Activities that were once exciting like checking out the open air market to shop for fresh fruits and vegetables is now just a weekly food shopping activity and ambiance plays second fiddle to functionality. Even now as we look out the windows of our incredible apartment in Montepulciano, Italy and see the rolling hills of the Tuscan countryside, we comment on the beauty but the moment does not take our breath away as it might have two months ago. It's an interesting thought that maybe the number of moments that take your breath away are inversely proportional to the number of special moments you have exposure to in any given period of time.

At this point we are all feeling a little travel weary. It's not homesickness, as I don't feel homesick in the least. It's more of a tiredness which breeds laziness. A feeling that sometimes seeing this sight or that sight requires more energy than I have at the moment and may just not be worth the effort. A feeling of been there/done that/let's move on. A friend asked in an email "Are you tired of being a tourist?" Maybe that's a good way of putting it. Some days we are just tired of being tourists.

Now understand, even though you read lots of blogs of our adventures, there are lots of days with no adventures. We call those "down days" or "in days." Days where we do laundry (which takes much longer here since the wash cycles go for about two hours), read, journal, blog, catch up on emails, edit pictures, tend to personal business and tend to present and future trip business. We even watch videos if we can find a video rental shop in town (we are card carrying members of a video rental shop ("The Music Box") in Ljubljana, Slovenia). We actually enjoy these days just as much as our "tourist" days and they give our life some sense of place. They also enable us to "renew" ourselves. At times we feel almost guilty when we take those days as we feel "Here we are in _____ (fill in the blank), we should go out and do or see something." But we quickly move on from those thoughts as we know that everyday can not be used for sightseeing. It's much easier to move on from that guilty feeling when we are in a given location for a longer period of time.

So with three months down and nine months to go, where do we go from here? Literally, to Rome. Emotionally, well, we're not sure. We're hoping that when we leave Europe in a little less than two weeks, there will be a renewed excitement as we hit the continent of Africa and experience something totally different than what we have had over the last three months. That difference will continue as we wind our way through India, Thailand, Laos and China. By the time we hit Australia and New Zealand, the "sameness" that we might experience might be a welcome relief.

Often My Own Emotions Surprised Me...

Wednesday, January 28, 2009
POST AFRICA/ASIA BLUES

Posted by lisa at 6:00 AM

After a big event in my life is over, I often get the blues.
You know what I mean, an event that required a lot of
planning, a lot of time, a lot of energy. Then you finally have
the event occur and afterwards you are left with a hole in
your schedule and a hole in your heart. That's where I am
now, feeling the aftermath of the planning and experiencing
of this whole round the world adventure. "But wait a minute"
I tell myself, "It's not over." "I am in Australia, the Land
Down Under. I am half way around the world; a 16 hour time
difference from EST in the US!" The problem is, it doesn't
feel that way!

Sydney is a great city, lots to do, easy to get around and
beautiful beaches. But everything is in English. The people
speak English, the signs are in English. Most people are white
and everyone wears Western clothes. I swear there are more
Thai restaurants in this city than there were in Thailand, but
when you walk in, no one says Sawaddeekaa, the traditional
Thai greeting. It doesn't feel like I'm home in Cincinnati, but
instead, vacationing, in let's say, California. It's nice here,
don't get me wrong, it's just that I miss the strange and
exotic.

I miss seeing the women of India in their bright and colorful
sarees walking down the street. Or the women of Africa in
their bold colored caftans and head wraps. I miss seeing
signs in languages I can't read or hearing people speak
languages I can't understand. The enthusiasm of trying to

learn at least a few words in a new language, and the success you feel when someone acknowledges your greeting and returns one to you. I miss riding in tuk-tuks which are a terribly uncomfortable ride but hey, they are different. You can get take away (take out to us Americans) here from most restaurants but it's not quite the same as eating some of the amazing street food that we had in Asia. I even miss being stared at and having people we don't know take our pictures. (I know that Avocet and Siena don't miss that)

Europe was "Western" as well but there was a different language to each country and food differences as well. The architecture was old and beautiful and each city we visited had its own version of European charm. Besides, Europe was at the beginning of our trip and everything was new and exciting. AND, we hadn't been to Africa and Asia yet!

The scary thing is, as the world becomes more Westernized (and it is, there is no doubt about that) where will we all go to experience something different? When a ten year old Chinese kid can speak English as well as a ten year old American kid, you know that soon, the whole world will be speaking English. Traditional dress will give way to Westernized clothes and Coca Cola won't be the only American product in people's kitchens.

For another six weeks we will be in Australia and New Zealand where the only thing strange and exotic will be the animals. I will have to find a way to get over my "Blues" and enjoy what both of these countries have to offer – I may never be back here again. After that, we move on to South America where everything will be in Spanish, people will look different and their culture will be unique. I will have three months to enjoy the differences until the "Real Blues" set in – the trip really will be over!

Chapter Twenty-Two

PLANES, TRAINS & AUTOMOBILES

Whether you first head east or west, chances are your first transportation will be a transoceanic flight. After that, all options are open as to how to get from point A to point B. As you explore your future transportation options consider your objectives:

- ➢ Transportation only
- ➢ Transportation along with sightseeing
- ➢ Reduced costs
- ➢ Time
- ➢ Convenience
- ➢ New experience/novelty

Planes

Planes offer transportation with no sightseeing options, unless you consider clouds or aerial views of mountains sightseeing. It is typically the quickest way to anywhere, especially if you are covering long distances. It tends to be the most costly but don't always assume that. Sometimes you can get discount flights that come in cheaper than other forms of transportation.

Look into both Round the World Tickets as well as segment tickets through a Round the World Broker. The second will give you much greater flexibility and may not be much more expensive than the first. These options will typically be for your long haul segments. Before you pick a Round the World Broker, shop around. It's not that they have access to substantially different prices as much as that they may route you differently which in the end will have an impact on cost. Our first long haul flight was from Rome to Arusha, Tanzania. (We had free tickets to Europe) One broker had us traveling: Rome - Nairobi, Kenya - Dar Es Salaam, Tanzania - Arusha. The other routed us from Rome - Doha, Qatar - Dar Es Salaam - Arusha. Both would get us to the same place, but by choosing the second routing, we saved $1200. It's easy to use multiple brokers in the early stages of planning since at that point, you're just shopping around. Once you start actually booking, however, it will be more difficult to continue to investigate your options. Brokers earn commissions off their sales. They are not going to want to keep supplying you information if it becomes clear you're not buying anything from them.

For shorter distances you will have to do your own research. There are many discount airlines to explore for shorter segments. Almost all of these can be booked online and often the "base" fare will be cheaper than other transportation options. Don't forget to look into country or area specific discount packages. In Southeast Asia we were able to use the Discovery Pass (Bangkok Air and Lao Aviation) which enabled us to pay a lower cost per leg if we purchased three or more legs in that area. It turned out to be a nice cost savings. I had trouble purchasing the Discovery Pass on my own, but my air broker was able to purchase if for us.

When comparing the cost effectiveness of these short haul flights to other forms of transportation, be sure to add in all the ala carte extras: flight taxes and surcharges, checked baggage costs, airport departure tax, transportation to and from the airport. Airports are typically out of town making them costly to get to. Train or bus stations are typically in town and can be reached easier and cheaper.

For a shorter trip, a flight may not always be the fastest. You first have to get to the airport. Then you have hours tied up in security and immigration. Once at your destination, you have to go through immigration again, gather your checked luggage, and get into the city which is probably another long distance from the airport.

Before booking any flights, don't forget those treasured Frequent Flyer Miles you have been accumulating. We often think of them as worthless since airlines keep changing the rules on us making them less and less valuable. But they do still work and may be able to save you some money. We were able to use our Delta Frequent Flyer Miles to get ourselves to our first destination, The Netherlands, saving us the expense of a transatlantic flight. We were not, however, able to get tickets from Cincinnati to Amsterdam as there were no frequent flyer seats available on those flights. Don't let that deter you. Get the agent to work backwards for you. What flight coming into Amsterdam on this date has frequent flyer seats available and from where? Marty was able to find seats on a flight out of Dallas/Ft. Worth. We then booked our flight from Cincinnati to Amsterdam, via Dallas/Ft. Worth. We had to stay overnight in Dallas which we deemed a small price to pay for free tickets.

Once you have booked your flights, don't consider it a done deal. Expect changes! Some will be minor, a flight leaving a half hour earlier or ten minutes later. But some can be significant. We had a flight into Hong Kong that moved forward two days. Two extra days in Hong Kong? Hong Kong is a very expensive city. Our budget wasn't going to allow for that. I emailed our air broker and discovered that Dragon Air had discontinued the flight from Guilin, China to Hong Kong on the day we were supposed to travel. The option was to leave two days earlier or one day later. Our agent made the executive decision for us to go earlier. I let him know that wouldn't work for us and had him schedule the later flight instead. When changes occur, look to see how these changes might impact other arrangements already in place. Do you need to change accommodation bookings? Have you arranged for a driver or a ride from the airport that needs to be informed of your new arrival time? Regardless of whether you have been informed of any changes, be sure to reconfirm your flights at least twenty-four hours in advance for every flight you are scheduled to take.

Over the course of the year we took thirty-two flights. This included all segments, sometimes taking multiple flights to get to a particular destination. Our longest flight was about ten hours and our shortest was twenty minutes. Most of our flights were long haul flights so they were the obvious choice but that was not always the case. Our twenty minute flight was from Zanzibar to Dar Es Saalem. We took a three hour ferry out to Zanzibar from DarEes Saalem, but upon our return, we needed to catch a flight to India. When you added up the cost of the ferry tickets, plus a cab to the airport (clear across town), it was cheaper to fly back and much more convenient.

We chose to fly from Amsterdam, The Netherlands to Krakow, Poland because it was cheaper than taking the train. But the flight from Arusha to Dar Es Saalem and another from Buenos Aires to Iguazu Falls were chosen strictly to avoid a long bus ride that would have made the girls and I motion sick.

When traveling with children, ask for a children's fare when booking. US domestic flights have no such fare category but that's not true of other carriers worldwide. Sometimes the fares are as low as 50% of an adult fare. Also, contact the airline ahead of time and ask for a child's meal. They'll get served before anyone else and there's a better chance they will be served food more to their liking. Even if they don't care for the food, it will be presented in a kid friendly manner so chances are your child will be more pleased than with an adult meal. It also alerts the flight crew that your children are on board. Often they're offered activity kits, backpacks or some gift item they will enjoy receiving.

Trains

Trains are a great way to travel and one of the safest, but not necessarily the cheapest, particularly in Europe. If there are just one or two of you traveling, it might prove to be economical. But when you multiply fares times four, often it's cheaper to rent a car. Train stations are typically close to town and can often be walked to or accessed by a quick bus or taxi ride. If you're traveling during the day, you might catch some great views of smaller towns or the countryside and you may have the opportunity to break down a longer trip into shorter segments in order to take in some sights along the way. You can cover a long distance in a decent amount of time and for those of us who get motion sick, trains are often one of those modes of transportation that spare us our discomfort. Avocet, Siena and I can all read on a train, whereas we can't in a car or bus.

I grew up on the east coast of the US so trains are not foreign to me. But to my husband and children who grew up in the Midwest, trains are a new and different mode of transportation; and an overnight train an even greater novelty. If schedules work out, an overnight train can be a way to save time and money. Traveling at night gives you a full day in your current location and then, when you wake up the next morning, a full day in your new location. While you pay more for a sleeping compartment, if you consider it is both your transportation and accommodation, you will find it is a cost saver.

You can obtain English Language train schedules for almost anywhere around the world on the Internet. This allows you to plan departures and arrivals in advance. Check out Seat61.com. Here you can find all the information you need: schedules, fares, route information, how to purchase a ticket in advance and recommendations on which tickets should be purchased ahead. And, it's all in English! It's not always easy booking in advance but it does assure you tickets (especially for sleeper cars) on heavily trafficked routes prior to even arriving in that country. While in Croatia we obtained round trip tickets for the overnight train from Delhi to Pathankot, India and while in Italy, we purchased overnight train tickets from Bangkok to Chiang Mai, Thailand. We had previously read that tickets for both these routes could be difficult to obtain if we waited until the last minute.

Most countries have multiple sleeping options on trains. First class gives you a separate locking compartment and air conditioning. Second class is cheaper and probably just as sufficient for sleeping purposes, but you don't have a separate compartment. The kids probably would have slept fine in second class, but Marty and I figured we'd never get any sleep if we were always worried about our luggage, so we always opted for first class. If you are traveling alone, first class would be very costly as you would need to purchase the whole compartment (which sleeps two) in order to have the "full security" first class offers. On the other hand, is exposing your luggage to just one stranger better than exposing it to the hoards of people on the train? If you choose to go second class, be sure you have a good lock on your luggage and, if possible, a way to lock the bag itself to the seat. Can't decide whether to spring for first class or not, check out seat61.com for the lowdown. The site gives detailed information on the sleeping situation including pictures. Traveling with children? Ask for a four person compartment or connecting compartments (two individual compartments with a door in between). I can't speak for all trains or for all countries, but in both countries where we took overnight trains, India and Thailand, we were able to get one of these two options on all four overnight trains.

While there is food and water available on the train, it's a good idea to take your own food and water in your day pack. What is served on the train may not be to your liking, served exactly when you want it, or meet the health standards you are trying to maintain. If you are not a good sleeper, OTC sleeping pills and ear plugs might go a long way toward helping you get a better night's sleep.

Ferries

Sometimes you can't get from point A to point B by land, so your options are by air or by sea. Like a train, a ferry is an alternative to air travel and offers you the opportunity to have a different experience. Sometimes it offers beautiful views like when we ferried up the coast of Croatia. Other times, it is strictly transportation as all there is to see is water and more water. It tends to be a convenient form of transportation as the port is typically close to the city and long distance trips can often be broken up into shorter segments for additional sightseeing opportunities. Costs will obviously vary a great deal but it will most likely be cheaper than air travel.

Overnight ferries, like overnight trains, offer both transportation and accommodations, giving you a potential cost savings. We were trying to get from Korcula, Croatia to Ljubljana, Slovenia. The plan was to go overland from Korcula to Zagreb, via Split, using a local ferry, a bus and a train and then another train across the boarder into Slovenia. The trip from Korcula to Zagreb was long so we figured we should spend the night in Zagreb prior to moving on. Aside from a long overland trip and the costs associated with it, the hotels in Zagreb were very expensive. Since Zagreb was not a destination city for us, we decided to bypass it, taking the overnight ferry from Korcula, up the cost of Croatia to the city of Rijeka. From there we could catch a bus to Ljubljana. The trip ended up being easier, cheaper and a great cultural experience. We met a lovely mother/daughter travel duo from Australia, watched some young adults play scrabble in Slovene, listened to a couple of gypsies play some awesome violin music (probably earning enough in tips to pay their ferry fare) and heard a young man sing a beautiful aria. We observed the backpackers as they maneuvered for the best sleeping spots.

You can spring for a sleeping compartment and actually sleep on a bed (small, but a bed none the less) or you can do like many people do and just stake out an area for yourself on deck or inside one of the lounges. As with the train, if you have a compartment, you not only have privacy, you have a locked area in which to store your luggage. If you sleep out in the open, you need to sleep with one eye open in order to watch your belongings. Prior to taking an overnight ferry, I would have thought that the open areas were pretty much occupied by backpackers but that's not the case. We saw plenty of couples and even families take advantage of the cheaper rates of not having an overnight compartment. If you chose this route, be sure to get onto the ferry as fast as possible as the "good spots" go very quickly.

Like trains, ferries run on a schedule so you will need to check out the time table as you make your plans. Short haul ferries may run multiple times a day but longer haul ferries may run only once a day or possibly only several times a week. In addition, ferries often run seasonally. In high season, they may run more frequently; in low season, sporadically or possibly not at all. Bring food, water, OTC sleeping pills, ear plugs and, if you get sea sick, some Dramamine.

Buses

Other than local buses, we didn't use this form of transportation much. When you get motion sick, bus travel is not the first choice for longer hauls. If you don't get sick, however, bus travel is a great way to see more of a country and at a reduced cost. In most countries, bus travel is incredibly inexpensive, often on buses that are quite luxurious. We were talking with a woman who had taken the sixteen hour bus ride from Buenos Aires to Iguazu Falls who raved about her trip. She said the seats folded down completely into a bed and that it was quite comfortable – of course, she was half my age which might have had something to do with that! Bus stations are typically in or close to the center of town and are therefore easy and inexpensive to get to. And, you have the ability to get on and off the bus at interim stops or to break a long trip into several smaller trips. This creates ample sightseeing opportunities in between destination cities. The downfalls are safety and the time factor involved. Buses in many countries are not considered as safe as other forms of transportation so you should look into a particular country's reputation for safety prior to planning any long haul bus travel. If the risks seem reasonable and time is on your side, bus travel is certainly worth a try.

How nice a bus you have and the amenities you're offered will vary from country to country. Always ask questions before booking and don't assume anything. Just because it's a seven hour trip doesn't mean there will be a toilet on the bus. The trip from Luang Prabang to Laos' capital, Vientiene is suppose to be an incredibly beautiful ride, but the bathroom facilities are the bushes on the side of the road, not a little room in the back of the bus. Be sure to bring your own food and water for the trip – don't count on a stop to pick up provisions.

Automobiles

Chances are, if you're an American, you use a car to get from one place to another more than any other mode of transportation. Not just on a daily basis, but even on vacation. If we're not taking a driving vacation in our own car, often we rent a car after taking a flight to get to our destination. Having a car is the ultimate in convenience: it goes when you want it to go, stops when you want it to stop, pulls right up to your door (almost) and you can change your mind and direction on a dime. If you are only one person traveling, the cost of a rental car and gas will be high. But, if you are a group or a family of four, there's a chance it might be cheaper than alternative forms of transportation.

We rented a car a total of twelve times. Nine of those times were one day rentals for a day trip, while the other three times were for a week or longer. When we rented a car for a day trip it was for all the obvious reasons. We could leave and return on our schedule and make stops along the way visiting sights in between our two destination points. It was the quickest, easiest and often the only way to get to a particular destination. Sometimes it was also the cheapest. The other three times we rented a car was due to location. It's hard to tour Tuscany, visiting all the lovely hill towns, without a car. Not impossible, but challenging. In Tasmania, Australia and Rotorua, New Zealand,

194

our week long stays would have been impossible without the use of a car.

When renting a car, check around as rates can vary significantly. Though not required in all countries, it is still recommended that you have an international driving permit (IDP). You can obtain an IDP from your local American Automobile Association (AAA) office or the American Automobile Touring Alliance. These two associations are the only authorized distributors of IDPs in the United States. Even with an international driving permit, you will need your state driver's license, as well as your passport, when renting a car.

For car buffs out there, like my husband, renting a car gives you the opportunity to drive cars that are not available here in the United States. While we weren't able to drive some of those tiny cars in Europe that look more like Cozy Coupes than cars (hard to fit four people into any of those), we were able to rent some fine, energy efficient cars, unique to those countries. Not a big thrill for me or the girls, but Marty was in seventh heaven.

One thing you will miss by renting your own vehicle are opportunities to meet other people. Public transportation is a great way to interact with both locals and other travelers. We had superb conversations on planes, trains, buses and ferries. We picked up everything from local history and customs to travel tips for the present and future. In the car, you are going to be talking to the same people you have been talking with for the last _____ (fill in the blank) days!

Before renting a vehicle, consider everything before deciding it's the right way to go:

- ➢ Where are you going to park when you get to your destination and how much will it cost?
- ➢ If the rental is for more than a day, where will you park in the evening near your accommodation and how much will that cost?
- ➢ Are the road signs in English or will you have trouble navigating around the city?
- ➢ Which side of the road will you be driving on and can you comfortably and safely adjust to that change?
- ➢ Will you have a navigator to help you? What is traffic like in the city in which you are traveling?

> ➢ Will it be easier to take public transportation than sit in bumper to bumper traffic?
> ➢ Exactly how much is fuel per gallon once you calculate the exchange rate and convert from liters to gallons?

When renting a car, be sure to leave the car rental office with a really good map.

If you are stepping off a long flight that crossed multiple time zones, consider picking up your car several days later rather than upon your arrival. Road accidents are the number one danger to travelers and adding jet lag into the mix is not a good idea. Wait until you have adequately adjusted to your new time zone before getting behind the wheel of a car. It's also a good idea to restrict your auto travel to daytime hours, avoiding using roads at night. Aside from the obvious issues of vision and direction, in many countries, being on a road at night is just not safe. It's a good idea to have a passenger with you at all times to help you navigate, but at a minimum, the first few times driving in a new area. This will be especially helpful if you are new to driving on the left side of the road as your navigator can remind you of your new driving rules each time you make a turn (turn right, stay left or turn left, stay left). If driving a stick shift is not "automatic" to you, don't get one. You don't need one additional issue to concentrate on while traveling foreign roads. Don't talk on a cell phone while driving and lastly, allow time for mistakes – you will make them!

Drivers

Sometimes you desire all the conveniences of a car but don't want any of the hassles; you can solve this dilemma by hiring a driver. While this sounds like an expensive ordeal, in cheaper countries, it's not as costly as you might think. In fact, this is a very normal form of transportation in some parts of the world. Drivers can be hired for a day of sightseeing, picking you up at your accommodation in the morning and returning you back there at the end of a day. Or drivers can be hired for multiple days, taking you to different cities.

In India we opted to hire a driver for multiple situations. We contracted for a day in Delhi in order to see a number of sights we wanted to see that were spread pretty far apart. This same driver, Ranvir, picked us up at the train station in Delhi, a week later, and drove us to Jaipur - about a five hour drive from Delhi. After dropping us off at our hotel, he returned the next day to provide us with a day of sightseeing in Jaipur. Ranvir then left town and returned a week later to drive us to Agra to see the Taj Mahal. We overnighted in Agra, saw the Taj in the morning and then were met once again for a drive back to Delhi to catch our flight to Thailand.

Drivers can be a mixed blessing. On the one hand, you have a local at your disposal who knows the language, customs, directions and sights to see in the area. They watch not only the car, but also all of your belongings in the car, which will be everything if this is not a day trip. Chances are, they won't get lost, but if they do, they can more easily figure out how to get where they need to go than you. And, if they have an accident, it is a much smaller deal than if you have an accident as a foreigner.

On the other hand, they have their own agenda. Even though you're the one who is paying them, they will often want to do what they want to do, when they want to do it. In addition, only a small portion of their income comes from driving. A greater portion comes from commissions they make when customers are brought into shops with which they have arrangements. They will want to take you to their "brother's shop" in the hopes you buy something and they get additional funds. Even being very firm and insistent with them, you will find yourself in places you didn't particularly want to go. Consider it one of the hazards of this mode of transportation and try not to let it get the better of you.

Make sure the car that comes with the driver you hired is to your liking. In Delhi, they tried to put our family of four, with all our luggage, in a car way too small given the long drives ahead of us. We insisted on a bigger car, so they switched drivers and we had a much more comfortable ride. And just because you hired a driver for the day doesn't mean you have to keep him the whole day if you don't want to. Halfway through our sightseeing day in Jaipur, we wanted to get away from Ranvir and be on our own. We told him to drop us off at the City Palace and we would take care of our own transportation back.

Tip your driver. In the US, we tip for personal services and having a driver in a foreign country is certainly a personal service. You may not love your driver, but they are there for you. They count on this tip as a large percentage of their income so be as generous as you can. When your driver has been extra good or has gone out of his way for you, show your appreciation monetarily.

Bikes

Unless you are taking a biking holiday, chances are you're not going to be using bikes as a mode of transportation for any real distances. You may, however, be using it to get around town and a great mode it is. Riding a bike is faster than walking yet you still get to see all the local sights. It gives you an opportunity to get "your hands" around a city quickly and feel more like a local than a tourist.

Write down the names and addresses of several bike rental shops when doing your research. These types of shops are often tucked away so you won't just happen upon them walking around town. Even if you don't think you are going to want to bike ride, write the names down anyway. Once at that location, you might become interested and then you'll be one step ahead

We rented bikes in Krakow, Poland and Lucca, Italy and rode around the city on bike/walking paths and on ancient city walls. It was a fun way to explore the cities and spend an afternoon. In Yangshou, China, we rented bikes to go out into the countryside. We even crossed a river, with our bikes, on bamboo rafts – an experience to remember. In Nong Khai, Thailand we used bikes as transportation to go visit the incredible Salakaewkoo Sculpture Park. There we couldn't find children's bikes to rent. We eventually found a shop where a woman had a daughter about the same age as Siena and Avocet. She rented us her daughter's bike which the girls took turns riding while the other rode on the back of Marty's bike. All were adventures that added to our appreciation of the city as well as a greater understanding of its culture. Be sure to obtain a bicycle lock along with your rental.

If you are going to be in one location for any length of time, an alternative to a bike rental is a bike purchase. I'm not talking about a brand new bike, but a used bike. In Haarlem, The Netherlands, we wanted bikes. Not just bikes for a day but bikes for almost three weeks. Everyone in Holland rides bikes and we wanted to be part of that culture. We found plenty of places to rent adult bikes, but believe it or not, we couldn't find any kids' bikes to rent. We wandered into a new bike shop and asked if there was anywhere in town that might rent or even sell used children's bikes. He told us about Fietsco, a used bike shop, located just outside the downtown area. At Fietsco, we were able to buy four bikes as well as bike locks. Our total cost was less than what it would have cost to rent bikes for just one week, and we had our bikes for three weeks! When we were about to leave Haarlem, we brought our bikes back to Eelco at Fietsco. He not only bought our bikes back from us, but was even willing to give us something for the locks we had purchased. Not finding kids bikes to rent turned out to be the best thing that could have happened to us.

Having bikes in Holland was different than the other times we had bikes along the trip. In Holland, it was a way of life. We used our bikes everyday. Sometimes it was transportation to get to and from the train station or to the market to do our food shopping. Other times it was used as a day activity. Once we rode our bikes to Zandvort, a beach town on the North Sea, about fifteen kilometers away. It was the perfect way to feel Dutch.

If you do purchase a bike, or rent for a longer period of time, you will need to consider where you will store it. In Haarlem we had a house and we just kept the bikes inside. But other accommodations we rented were not as conducive to "having" a bike. If you obtain a good lock, there might be someplace outside your accommodation where you can store your bikes.

Scooters and Motorcycles

While not a form of transportation we used, scooters and motorcycles are a great way to get around. They are economical, environmentally sound, easy to park and move a whole lot faster than bicycles (at least at the rate I pedal). They are, however, not for the inexperienced. You won't have to look hard to find statistics showing the large number of accidents that occur on scooters and motorcycles driven by tourists. If you have used them before, by all means rent one and go out exploring. If you have never been on one, this is not the time to start. If you think you might want to do this while traveling, create an opportunity to experiment prior to leaving and see how quickly you adapt to it.

In Thailand, Siena and Avocet were anxious to ride on a scooter. Since I had never driven one, I wasn't about to risk my child's life, as well as my own, to make them happy. Marty, on the other hand, had driven a scooter before. He rented one for half a day and took turns taking the girls out one at a time. They kept to the smaller streets and had a safe and great time. Before our next trip I would like to learn how to ride one. They look like a lot of fun and are a superb way to explore the countryside where public transportation is not readily available.

Other Local Transportation

Whether it's local buses, subways, trolleys, tuk tuks, rickshaws, or collectivos, using local transportation is a superb way to experience the culture. Using any of these forms of transportation requires you to learn something: where to get on, where to get off, how the route operates, how to bargain for a fair fare and how to be safe. Sometimes you can get the needed information in advance while other times it's a matter of trial and error - all a part of travel. Trial and error, however, is not acceptable when it comes to safety. If other travelers warn you about a method of travel that is unsafe, objectively look at their warning. If you are told a particular subway stop is questionable, look to see if there is an alternative to that stop. Public transportation can be extremely crowded and is an ideal place to get ripped off and/or lose a child. Keep your eyes and hands on your belongings and your children, making sure you know where both are at all times!

Walking

I only have three words to say about walking. Walk, Walk, Walk. It is economical and the best way to take in everything: sights, sounds, smells, culture etc. You never know what you might miss if you take the subway from one end of town to the other, but if you walk, you'll take in everything. Walking is excellent exercise and will help you stay in better health during your trip. It will also enable you to eat some of the wonderful local cuisine and still be able to fit into the only clothes you have by the end of your trip.

How About This Form of Transportation...

Wednesday, September 3, 2008
<u>**GONDOLA Watch 101**</u>

Posted by Avocet and Siena at 6:00 AM

As said in Daddy's last blog, our flat has a large window overlooking a Gondola canal. As soon as we realized this, we immediately took to watching them go by. There were a surprising number of them, considering the high cost of a Gondola ride. After our first day, we started saying "Ciao!" to the Gondola drivers that passed by; not to the lucky people taking the ride. After that, we set up little stools everyday to say "Ciao" and watch the people go by. Siena and I called this Gondola Watch 101.

~written by Avocet

Before I write my part of this blog I would like you to take an Italian lesson.

Ciao-hello
Ciao Bella- hello beautiful
Ciao Amore- hello love

These were some of the responses from the Gondola drivers.

After we started to get used to Gondola Watch, whenever I saw a Gondola I would yell out to Avocet (or she would yell out to me) "Gondola Watch 101!!" and the other would come running. Then we would sit by the window and say "Ciao!" Sometimes the Gondola driver wouldn't say anything, and if this happened we would turn to each other and say M.O.M, which stands for, mean ol' man. Sometimes they would say

"Ciao" back, or sometimes they would say "Ciao Bella" or "Ciao Amore". We actually got to the point where we could recognize some of the Gondola drivers and after we said "Ciao" they would say "Ciao Ciao" or "Ciao Meow Meow". Some of the people riding in the Gondola would notice us too and say "Ciao" or sometimes take a picture of us!! When they said "Ciao" to us, we would always say to each other, "They're trying to act cool and Italian; the Gondola drivers are cool and Italian!" Some Gondolas have a hired accordion player and singer; once we heard someone singing Oh Solo Mio. Some people bring wine on the ride. It was fun to see the Gondolas go by and say "Ciao!"

Written by~ Siena

P.S. If you would like to hear Oh Solo Mio, go to www.youtube.com and key in Oh Solo Mio in the toolbar.

Chapter Twenty-Three

ALL ABOUT KIDS

Issues addressed in this book are for all long term travelers, regardless of whether you are traveling alone, with a spouse or partner, or as a family. Having done this trip with children, however, warrants at least one chapter unto itself.

There is no doubt in my mind (or Marty's) that this trip would have been a lot easier to take by ourselves i.e. sans children. Not only that, it would have been a lot cheaper too! Two airfares versus four would have been an incredible cost savings alone without having to look any further. But we didn't! And the reasons for that vary from the selfish to the selfless.

We didn't want to wait. We wanted to take this trip now: before we were too old, before we were no longer physically able to, before something happened to one of us that would prevent us from ever taking a trip of this magnitude. The "Why put off until tomorrow what you can do today approach." I know people who would take our children for an overnight, maybe even a weekend, but I don't know anyone who would take our kids (or anyone else's for that matter) for a full year! And, of course, we wouldn't want to be away from them that long even if someone did offer. If we wanted to take this trip now, it was going to have to be a foursome, not a twosome.

We thought about what a life changing trip this would be. Marty and I have less than half our lives ahead of us at this point, but our children, have their <u>whole</u> lives ahead of them. This trip would have a major impact on their futures both in terms of who they are and what they will do with their lives. What a gift to give to them even if they can't fully appreciate the magnitude of the gift at this point. I would have liked to have been on the receiving end of a gift like this when I was a child, and I know we wanted to be on the giving end of this type of gift as parents. We have no control over our children's future, but we can give them a big canvas with the largest array of colors possible so that they can paint their lives with reckless abandon.

And having been children ourselves once, Marty and I knew it wouldn't be long before the opportunity to create family bonding experiences would be few and far between. Avocet and Siena, hitting their tween years, would soon be more interested in spending time with their friends than they would with us. Certainly taking a trip around the world would mean going out with a bang in terms of creating lasting family memories.

There's a lot more work in the preparation if you are planning on taking a family. You have to purchase items and pack for additional people. You are also looking for accommodations to house more people which is more challenging; it's easier to find accommodations for two than it is for four. We felt a greater need to have more planned in advance because we were traveling with our children; you therefore have more upfront work to do before you leave. No one ever said having children was easy and if you already have some, you know a family is a lot of work no matter where you are. If you want to take this trip as a family, you accept the additional work as part of the package.

How did the kids do? Incredible! They had their moments, but they would have had those at home too, just about different things. They got homesick at times and at times wanted to stop traveling, but they persevered. They were absolutely amazing at keeping themselves entertained, finding all kinds of ways to play with whatever happened to be available to them at the time. Sometimes they were so into where we were that they took over planning for the day. In Ljubljana, Slovenia we went on a tour of the architect, Joze Plecnik's, house. He was a prominent figure in designing the city. Several days later, the girls created the Plecnik Tour where they led us around the city pointing out the buildings that Plecnik designed along with their key architectural features. (see Plecnik – Ljubljana's Greatest Architect, August 20, 2008 at Oneworldonetrip.blogspot.com).

One of our biggest fears in traveling with the kids was the issue of food. If we had two adventurous eaters, the thought may never have crossed our minds. But we have only one semi-adventurous eater. The other is what you would call "picky." Actually, she's beyond picky. She's a vegetarian (since birth) who eats almost no vegetables and few fruits. She has a keen sense of smell and is highly sensitive to textures. Because of this, she tries very few new things, particularly if they don't smell or look good to her. Eating in a restaurant here in American is challenging, so whatever made us think we could take her on a trip around the world and not have her suffer from malnutrition? We just did! We figured somehow we could make it work.

The security blanket for the food issue was the jar of peanut butter Avocet perpetually carried. We left home with one packed in her suitcase (in one of those precious Ziploc bags). If food of interest was discovered, the peanut butter wasn't touched. It was also not finished until it was known that it could be replaced with a country's own local version. We may not have always been able to say hello or good-bye in a given language, but we always managed to learn how to say peanut butter. We were ultimately able to purchase peanut butter in fifteen out of seventeen countries; no peanut butter was ever discovered in Argentina or Uruguay.

Avocet would have found it emotionally difficult to make the trip without the peanut butter, but physically, she could have. In addition to finding foods she was familiar with and liked, at least one or two new things were discovered in each country that she could enjoy: gouda cheese and Dutch pancakes in Holland, pierogies and potato pancakes in Poland, boreks in Croatia and Slovenia, momos in India and cheese empanadas in Chile to name a few. This is not to say there weren't challenging times and some restaurants were passed over because we couldn't find something Avocet would eat; but she made it and we all survived. Whatever fears or concerns might creep up for you, they are not insurmountable.

The only thing I would do differently with respect to the food issue is not to give into it as much as we did. Next time, a jar of peanut butter and some bread go into the day pack each day and if we all want to eat in a restaurant, Avocet will have to rely on her security blanket. This would have been a better solution than searching for a restaurant that made her happy, often at the sacrifice of others. If we chose this option two times in a row, on the third time, we would choose a place to her liking so she didn't feel totally ostracized.

It would have been a different trip had it been just Marty and I. There are things we would have done we just didn't do. But the reverse is also true. Having the kids along encouraged us to do things just the two of us would not have chosen and those things enriched our experience. In Chiang Mai, Thailand, the girls saw a brochure for Flight of the Gibbon. It's one of those rainforest adventures where you harness yourself up and swing on ziplines through the rainforest. They thought it would be lots of fun; I thought it would be a nightmare! I pushed myself to do it for their sake, had a great time, and achieved a little self growth along the way as I worked through my fears about stepping out without a safety net. (see Flight of the Gibbon, November 23, 2009 at Oneworldonetrip.blogspot.com). The girls also really enjoy horseback riding which is something Marty and I don't pursue. We went riding three times during the trip, but the most memorable one was riding through the sand dunes and on the beach outside of Valpariso, Chile. (see The Best Horseback Ride Ever, April 5, 2009 at Oneworldonetrip.blogspot.com). Riding through those miles of dunes with my family silhouetted against the sand is an experience I will never forget. If it weren't for my children, I never would have that memory. Every time you give something up by having your children along, you gain something on the other side. They will bring you to wonderful places and new adventures you hadn't even thought of.

Siena and Avocet did not want to go on this trip! They had heard about this trip for over two years. They knew it was part of their future, but there wasn't buy in. They couldn't understand why they should have to give up everything they have come to know and love (with the exception of their immediate family) for the unknown. "Just go without me!" Siena shouted one day as she was stressing out over missing the American Girl "Kit" movie that was coming out the summer we would be gone. A trip around the world versus a movie? It hardly seemed worth my time to think about. But, I knew, it was very real to her and shouldn't be dismissed. While both Marty and I knew in our hearts this would be a great experience for them, it didn't come without heartaches, especially during those few months prior to leaving when they voiced their negative feelings regarding this trip loud and clear.

I figured it would be years before they could fully appreciate the trip and equally as many years, before they would ever say thank you. But we didn't have to wait that long after all. One day in Haarlem, our very first stop, Avocet turned to me and said, "Thanks for dragging me on this trip." I thought I had died and gone to heaven. Multiple times throughout the trip we heard one or the other express gratitude for what we were doing. I still don't believe they have a full appreciation of what they have experienced, but, at age ten, I don't think they have the capacity to do so. We hope, sometime in the future, they will.

The lack of interaction with other children over the course of the year was a disappointment for us all. We thought they would come into contact with more children than they did. Either school calendars were in conflict with our itinerary so children were not around during the day, or the language barrier was just too much for them to cope with. Because of this, they became quite adept at conversations with adults. They too got tired of talking to just us or to each other, so in an effort to diversify their social life, it was interact with adults or nothing. By the end of the trip, I feared they would no longer be able to relate to their peers when they returned home. Silly me to have worried about such a thing. Within days of being home they were back to playing with their friends, never missing a beat. Children are so "in the moment" and adaptable to their environment.

Still, if they had not had each other, the trip would have been next to impossible. They were not only sisters, they were each other's sole playmate over the course of the year. Avocet and Siena got along fabulously with each other with little to no fighting or disagreeing. This, however, was not unique to the trip. At home they get along great as well. Making this trip with an only child would not be impossible, but it certainly would be challenging and I'm not sure I would have been up to the task. Even with multiple children, you will have to evaluate their relationship with each other to see if this is something that will work for your family. It could be that it would work, just not for quite as long as a year. Or it could turn out, based on your children's relationship with each other, that you might just wait until they all go off to college before you attempt a trip of this kind.

Something I was totally surprised at was the kids' attitude toward the trip once we got home. I know children are wonderful about living in the present so I anticipated that once they were back home physically, they would be back home mentally as well. I assumed the trip would be a memory they would share with others over time, the same as us. But that's not happening. They just don't talk about it. Both Siena and Avocet started a new school when we got back so none of their teachers or classmates knew them to be missing for a year. And now that they're in school, their teachers and classmates still don't know. It's one of our children's best kept secrets. When their social studies teacher observed their excellent geography skills, she asked them where they went to school last year. They both lied and told her that they went to the same school that they had attended for kindergarten through third grade. Neither had disclosed the true source of their great geography skills. I've asked if they are ashamed or embarrassed by the trip and they say "no." They tell me they just don't like to answer a lot of questions. I'm thinking it's all about fitting in. At this age, all kids just want to fit in. They want to be like everyone else. If they don't tell anyone they went around the world, then they will be just like everyone else. I don't mind that they've chosen not to share this information with others. It isn't necessary for them to brag or to place themselves above others because of what they have done. On the other hand, it makes me sad that fitting in is so important that children have to hide who they really are and pretend to be someone they're not. It also concerns me that they will lose the lessons of the "gift" they have received if they are not willing to even acknowledge they have received the gift in the first place. Only time will sort this one out.

This was a Sticky Situation...

Tuesday, June 10, 2008
THE PEANUT BUTTER INCIDENT
Posted by Avocet at 5:54 PM

Peanut Butter is very important to me. You see, I am a very picky eater and Peanut Butter is my main source of protein. One of the things I was worried about on the trip was food. I don't try new foods very easily and usually, I don't like the foods I do try. So I was bringing a jar of Trader Joes Creamy Peanut Butter. We were going to see how far I could go without opening the Peanut Butter. I thought I would start using it in Tanzania. When we went through security at the airport to get to our plane to Dallas Fort Worth, the evil security man didn't give me back my backpack right away even though I told him it was mine. When my mom came over, he asked if the backpack was mine. I said it was. Then he said something about having liquids in there. He started digging around in **my** backpack and soon discovered the jar of Peanut Butter. He said I couldn't take it and I could only take it if it was in my suitcase which, for your information, was already checked in. So he took away the jar and put it behind the counter. I was sad the **whole** plane ride. When we got to Dallas Fort Worth, we ate lunch at Denny's and then stopped in at the Shell gas station convenience store and picked up a jar of Peter Pan Crunchy Peanut Butter. It wasn't quite the same but then again, I have Peanut Butter again!!! (And this time, it goes in my suitcase!!!)

210

Chapter Twenty-Four

EMOTIONAL ROLLER COASTER III

Life was exciting and different while we were traveling. Not that we didn't have days that were mundane, but mostly everything was new and different. Now, back at home, everything is pretty much the same and it feels boring. Even things we once did for enjoyment don't have the same pizazz they used to. Yes, this Saturday we could go to our local art museum, but after having seen the great museums of the world, the local museum isn't all that exciting. Instead we could go to the park. But after trekking in the Andes Mountains, thoughts of the local park aren't motivating us to get out of bed in the morning. Like adventure "addicts" who are always looking for the next bigger, better, more outrageous adventure activity, we now feel like we need something more exciting and more exotic than the sights of our home town.

For the last month or so of life on the road we found ourselves living in two worlds once again. While we were present with our travels, we found ourselves thinking ahead about home. We were making "To Do" lists of things that needed to be taken care of upon our arrival. Even more proactive, we found ourselves actually doing things from the road in preparation for our return.

We felt a little cheated when it came to our last month of travel; that our experience was somehow lessened by the perpetual infiltration of thoughts of home. But we came to understand that we're only human and it would be pretty impossible to keep home and its related issues out of our lives forever. We wrote down what we needed to write down, did what we needed to do, and focused on keeping "home" out of our minds the rest of the time in order to enjoy the last of our traveling days. As anxious and preoccupied as we all were about going home, we loved and had a wonderful last two weeks in Quito, Ecuador.

Upon arrival in Cincinnati, we were thrilled to be sleeping in our own beds again, eating foods we hadn't had in a long time, seeing friends and family and staying put in one location. On the other hand, there was this huge letdown. It's over! We made our dream come true, now what? What do we have to look forward to from this point on? It's like when Christmas is over, or that fiftieth birthday bash, or the wedding that has been part of your life for 1½ years.

We were back to our normal, routine life. But to make matters worse, this normal, routine life that we came back to went on without us in our absence. Friends and family moved on while we were gone and now we have to figure out where and how we fit in. They are all the same people but are we? Will the same social contacts be rewarding to us or will we need new ones to fit who we are now?

Remember back in Emotional Roller Coaster I I talked about how special we felt by what we were about to do? Well, we did it. And guess what? We're no longer special. Inside we are and always will be. But on the outside, our lives now look the same as everyone else's. Unless we start walking around in t-shits that read "I went around the world last year, ask me about it," no one we meet is going to know about it. And what about the people that already knew about the trip; our friends and family who were so curious prior to our leaving? Well, they read our blog along the way, they looked at the pictures we shared and now they are ready to move on. They ask "So, how was it?" and other general questions, but the conversations are typically short and move on to the next topic quickly. We know they're not being rude and uncaring, it's just that what we did is not part of who they are and what their life is about. So we no longer feel special or unique, we mostly feel lonely. Lonely for the type of people we met on the road. Because while we were having this amazing adventure, they too were having their own amazing adventure and we shared a bond that is only shared with other travelers.

Life on the road was not stress free. But the stressors we experienced on the road were different than the stressors we experience in our day to day life at home. Not only are they different here, but there seems to be a lot more of them - coming

212

at you all day long! We coped with them in the past and we'll cope with them now. But having seen the other side, I'm not sure I want to keep grappling with them. Having had a glimpse of a different lifestyle, a more balanced lifestyle, makes me want to live differently.

We are different people, how can we not be? But sorting all this out is difficult. We've changed but we're not sure how. We know we want our life to look different than it looked before, but we're not quite sure what we want it to be or how to make it look that way once we figure it out. Life feels a bit in limbo and limbo is just not a comfortable place to be. Discomfort, however, is the precursor to change and we'll learn to sit with the discomfort, even embrace it, until change makes its grand entrance.

In the weeks and months after we first got home, we felt as if our family was falling apart. I would go for long walks, BY MYSELF, while the kids sequestered themselves to their rooms to read, BY THEMSELVES, while Marty tended to the yard, BY HIMSELF. What happened to this incredible bonding experience we just had? Was it a figment of our imaginations? No, but after being with each other ALL THE TIME for an entire year, we were very ready to separate; to have space and to do something on our own without regard for each other. The pendulum often swings in the opposite direction before it finds its center point.

Life Isn't as Simple Back In the USA...

Saturday, May 23, 2009
<u>HOME SWEET ALMOST HOME</u>
Posted by lisa at 9:44 PM

We arrived at Miami International Airport on Wednesday, May 20th. If you have to arrive in the US from South America, Miami is the place to go. The culture shock is minimized by the fact that everything is still in Spanish. We knew exactly where to enter (entrada), where to exit (salida) and where to go to the bathroom (banos). Very comforting!

I imagined the first picture in our return photo album to be the one from the airport that said Welcome to the United States of America. But there was no sign to take a picture of. I don't understand. We had one that said Bienvenidos Ecuador, Bienvenidos Uruguay... where was the one for the USA? Given the fact that we were arriving in Miami, I would have been happy with Bienvenidos Estados Unidos, but nothing. Are we really that unwelcoming?

We collected our luggage, proceeded through immigration and customs and headed over to Avis to get the rental car that would take us to Sun City Center (250 miles northwest) where my mother lives. I had reserved a full size car which would be the largest vehicle we've been in for a year, but we wanted to be comfortable for our five hour trip. When I checked in, Darleen, our faithful Avis representative, wanted to know if we wanted to upgrade to an SUV. No, the full size is fine. Do you want a GPS system? No thanks, not necessary. How about a DVD player for the kids? An insurance package? A fuel package? I JUST WANT A CAR! TRANSPORTATION! SOMETHING A LITTLE LARGER THAN A TUK-TUK!

Needing to refuel the car (since I didn't get that fuel package), I pull up to the pump at the gas station. Do I want to pay cash or credit? I put my credit card into the pump. What is my zip code? Do I want a receipt? Do I want a car wash? I JUST WANT GAS!

The next day, we take my mom shopping for a table and chairs for her new home. We picked out a lovely set and when I go to pay, the cashier wants to know if I am going to pay with cash or credit? Do I want to open a new credit account with Pier One and get a 10% discount? Do I want to be on their email list? I JUST WANT TO MAKE MY PURCHASE!

After having traveled the world for the past year I have come to see that America is the land of choices. But after having lived without all those choices for a year, I realize that I really didn't miss having them. In fact, life was a whole lot simpler when there was no choice. Didn't I feel deprived? No, not really. Has our quality of life really improved with all the choices that we have or has it just gotten more complicated? More time consuming? More confusing?

When I ask myself "How has this trip changed me?" I guess my first response is, "It has made me want to have a simpler life." But I'm back here in America so wish me luck.

Chapter Twenty-Five

IN THE END

We came home and settled in. We have personal journals documenting our thoughts and feelings of the incredible odyssey we have just taken. Our computer and/or online storage site holds 10,000+ pictures that we have no idea what to do with, but we figure time will sort that one out. The blog we wrote as a collective memento of our family's experience has been bound into a book which sits on our living room coffee table and is perused on occasion to reconfirm it was not all some very vivid dream.

But there's more - there's so much more...

We just had the most incredible human experience. We met people from all over the world. They spoke a different language, ate different foods, practiced different religions and lived a different culture and were all wonderful human beings. The acts of kindness shown to us never ceased to amaze me. When we were in Nong Khai, Thailand, bicycling to the sculpture park, we got lost. A man, a total stranger, jumped on his scooter and gave us an escort all the way to where we were going. He spoke not one word of English and we knew only thank you in Thai. This is but one example. I could fill a book with stories of people helping us or extending themselves to make our lives easier or more fulfilled. It's not that people at home aren't nice. It's that we aren't often in a position to receive kindnesses repeatedly when we are in our own environment. Step out into the world and you discover it is filled with wonderful people.

We live in a cynical world and trust is often hard to come by. Even when you want to trust, doubt seeps in, invading our true desire. I often find myself irritated that I don't feel I can count on somebody's words or actions. But when you are on the road, sometimes trust is all you have. The day before each flight, we would make arrangements for a driver to pick us up to take us to the airport. And on the day of the flight, we would sit there with our luggage, figuring out Plan B in case they didn't show up. We never enacted a Plan B! Every time somebody said they would be there, they were. Now that I'm back at home, I find myself slipping back to my old ways. I replay in my mind some of those incidents from our year of travel and tell myself it's OK to trust in the situation.

There are lessons to be learned from almost anything we do in our lives, but when you travel, the opportunities for these life lessons seem to occur with a greater frequency. My daughter just called from school ten minutes ago (literally). She was panicked because she had lost something at school that she needed today. The tears were flowing and I knew she wasn't able to think clearly in that frazzled state. I reminded her of the time she and her sister got locked in the bathroom in our apartment in Krakow, Poland. We were able to figure out a way to get them out because they remained calm. She took some breaths, calmed herself and then we were able to solve the problem at hand. Traveling can put you into some precarious situations, but you survive them. From that you are able to build up a reservoir of invincibility. "If I can survive that situation in India, I can certainly get through this." All of us have very full reservoirs at this point in our lives.

If you ever dreamed of a simpler life, this is your opportunity to experience it. Imagine a life where you have almost no schedule to keep; days where you don't have to be anyplace at any particular time. No phone, answering machine, door bell, mobile phone, mail or anyway for anyone to get hold of you other than email (and even that's not a guarantee). You have almost no household responsibilities and you don't have a car to maintain. The list goes on and on. It's not realistic to think you can live the rest of your life this way, but it gives you much to think about when you return home to your overly busy life. Balance is something we tried, as a family, to achieve in our life before we left, but until we took this trip, we really didn't know what balance was. Now that we've had a glimpse of the other side, we have a lot more to strive for with respect to a more balanced life here at home.

The simplicity issue doesn't stop there. It seemed every where in the world we went, life was simpler. In America we have "Freedom of Choice." But what the advertising industry calls freedom of choice, I have come to think of as a bombardment of choice. When I needed to buy toilet paper on the road, I went into the market and bought one of several brands of toilet paper. I didn't feel deprived that I didn't have 75 options to choose from: one ply or two, scented or unscented, single roll, double roll or jumbo roll, four pack, eight pack, sixteen pack or the family pack... Actually, I felt grateful I could just go into the store and buy toilet paper without really having to think about it. It's that way with everything. The multitude of decisions we are saddled with over the course of the day is sometimes unbearable. Unbearable and unnecessary. This isn't freedom. Freedom should feel lighter, easier and well, freer. To me it feels like more work, more responsibility and more decisions than we really need. Simplifying our lives in this materialistic world is going to be very challenging, but it's certainly one of our goals over the years ahead.

Returning home after a year abroad has a way of putting life into a different perspective. Things that were once important no longer seem important – be it material possessions or ways in which we lived our lives. And other aspects of our life which maybe were given less focus in the past, suddenly take on a higher priority. This doesn't mean we disposed of our old lifestyle overnight for a new one. It means our future might look different from our past as we make very conscious changes in the way we live our lives.

During these times when books like Eckart Tolle's, <u>The Power of Now</u>, are all the rage and phrases like "Being Present" are buzz words, doing something where you really are living in the present is not just giving lip service to the idea. Having a lifestyle where you are living day to day is a unique experience in today's world. You are not living with a "To Do" list of things that need to be done over the course of the week. Your calendar is not staring you in the face with seasonal obligations looming in the months ahead. For the most part, each day is what it is, a day to be enjoyed and treasured whatever you choose to do with it. When you are standing in front of the Taj Mahal, you are with that magnificent building and nothing else. And when you are curled up in your living room reading, you are with your book and the warmth of your family around you. We had our moments of multitasking and not being fully present with what we were doing, but it was much easier being with the moment in our year of traveling than in our over burdened lives at home. Just as with the simplicity issue, incorporating a sense of presence into our lives now that we are back will be challenging

If I had to pick one thing that existed in other places, that I would like to have here at home, it would have to be a greater sense of community. Here in America, we tend to live relatively solitary lives. Most of us have spacious homes or apartments where we spend the majority of our time. When it is cold outside, we go into our warm homes. When it is hot outside, we go into our air conditioning. We entertain ourselves with various electronic devices and on occasion, get together with friends.

Elsewhere, it seems, people come first. People's homes are smaller so they look to outdoor spaces as extensions of their smaller homes. People congregate in parks, plazas, pedestrian streets, to talk, eat, for entertainment. On Mother's Day in Quito, Ecuador we spent the day in Parque Carolina. It was a lovely day and the park was packed. There were people everywhere: walking, running, playing ball, boating, picnicking, bicycling - everyone having a good time. A couple weeks after we got home, we decided to spend Father's Day in a similar manner. We loaded our bikes and picnic lunch into the car and drove to a park here in Cincinnati. It too was a lovely day and the park itself rivaled any park we had been to elsewhere in the world. It was missing only one thing. People! There was almost no one there!

We may be one of the richest societies in this world, but studies show we are also one of the loneliest. People are so busy, it's difficult finding time to get together. When they can find the time, they are either too tired or feel that getting together has to be this big ordeal which sounds like too much work; so they just stay at home and watch TV or a movie, and go to bed early. And then we wonder why life doesn't feel fulfilling or why we don't feel connected to one another.

All the thoughts that have come to me since we have been home, along with the ones that will continue to percolate over the months, maybe even years, ahead, are like the 10,000+ pictures sitting in our computer. I don't yet know what I'm going to do about either of them. But over time, answers will come. And won't it be wonderful when we have figured out a way to incorporate into our lives the gems brought back with us, from having traveled the world.

The End...Or the Beginning...

Tuesday, June 16, 2009
THE LAST BLOG (OR NOT)
Posted by lisa and Marty at 7:39 PM

In January 2006, three and one half years ago, I said to
Marty, "If we are ever going to take this trip, we had better
start planning it." At that point I really wasn't convinced
that this trip would ever occur but I was certain of one
thing, if we didn't start planning it, then for sure it would
never happen. Just thinking about it or even talking about it
was not going to make it a reality.

As we started to make plans in earnest, book flights, arrange
for accommodations, obtain visas...it became clear that this
trip was really going to happen - sort of. I still found myself
saying "We are PLANNING on taking a trip around the
world." It was so difficult for me to say "We ARE taking a
trip around the world." Even at this late date was I still
scared that it wasn't going to happen? Or, was I scared that
it really was going to happen?

Well, it did happen. Of course I don't need to tell you that,
you watched it unfold right here on this blog. And the most
amazing thing of the whole year was just that; that it did
happen. We took a dream and made it into a reality. We
didn't let the myriad of obstacles that could have gotten in
our way, get in our way. We didn't let the abundance of
emotional issues that surfaced stop us either.

Taking this trip was the biggest thing that I have ever done
in my life. And at this stage of my life, it may be the biggest

thing that I will ever do. The good, the bad and the ugly of it all doesn't really matter. Just having made the trip made it a huge success. It was empowering, it made me stronger and if I can do this, I can do anything - as long as I can hold onto this feeling.

Avocet and Siena are young; they have their whole lives ahead of them. They will probably do something that will surpass this experience. That's OK. This wasn't their gig, it was ours. For them, this was a gift. An opportunity to see a world greater than the microcosm in which they live. An opportunity to have a different perspective as they grow and mature. And an opportunity to have a lifetime of memories that they can share with us.

I will miss writing this blog. For over a year now, this has been an important part of my life. Whether you were a religious follower or one who just popped on for a peek now and then, I thank you. While we will always have this blog as a family memento, knowing you were out there reading and going with us on our journey, made it that much more enjoyable to write. It was a great ride and I'm glad you all came along.

lisa

For me too, this process feels like it started decades ago. At the beginning, the onset of the trip was a lifetime away. What I didn't think about was the end of the trip. You plan for the things that must be done, the itinerary, the visas, the accommodations, etc. Those are "easy" in the long haul to work on because there is an excitement, an anticipation...even though they felt "hard" at the time. Now, after 42,000+

miles, what is there to look forward to? We won't be doing this again, at least the way it was done the first time. Av and Si's next adventure will be one of their own, maybe backpacking in their early twenties. The old farts of the family, lisa and I, will do something travel related in the future but not soon. A year on the road takes it out of you. So what is the next frontier? Job? Career? New hobby? Volunteering? Green business? Astronaut? Run for President (not)?

I have discovered that the past year has reminded me that life is an adventure. It is too precious to not consider it so. I know that on the cusp of fifty five years of age that I don't have even forty good healthy years left. Doing something just to make money or to please someone or to conform...forget it. This year was the adventure of a lifetime. But maybe just one of the adventures. There are many more to come. It was a GREAT, GREAT year.

Marty

ACKNOWLEDGEMENTS

I would like to express my deepest appreciation to all of those who have helped make this book possible:

Harriet Werfel Edwards, my editor, who did her best to make a writer out of me.

Jonathan Eaton, who at dinner one night, casually threw out a title that, in the end, named this book.

Dave Gutmann, for his perseverance and help in the interior layout.

Alan Brown of Photonics, who kept me from pulling all my hair out while developing the cover design.

Donna Orbach, my sister, without whom this trip, to its completion, would not have been possible.

Freda Shusterman, my mother, for her continued support in everything I do.

Marty Greenwell, my husband, who braved this adventure with me.

Siena and Avocet Greenwell, my daughters, just for being who you are.

CPSIA information can be obtained at www.ICGtesting.com
Printed in the USA
LVOW121204261011

252036LV00026B/8/P